THE PHILOSOPHY OF WHITEHEAD

THE PHILOSOPHY
OF WHITEHEAD

BY

RASVIHARY DAS, M.A., Ph.D.

New York

RUSSELL & RUSSELL

1964

FIRST PUBLISHED IN 1928
REISSUED, 1964, BY RUSSELL & RUSSELL, INC.
L. C. CATALOG CARD NO: 64—11851

PRINTED IN THE UNITED STATES OF AMERICA

THIS BOOK IS GRATEFULLY DEDICATED

TO

MOTILAL MANECKCHAND, Esq.

FOUNDER OF

THE INDIAN INSTITUTE OF PHILOSOPHY,

AMALNER

CONTENTS

PREFACE

My primary object in writing the following pages was to make clear to myself the main philosophical ideas of Professor A. N. Whitehead, as they are presented in his three books, *Process and Reality, Adventures of Ideas,* and *Science and the Modern World.* I cannot pretend that I have understood every point in Professor Whitehead's philosophy, but I flatter myself to think that his main philosophical ideas, on the whole at least, have not escaped my comprehension. I have tried to present them as simply as I could in this book. I am not sure if I have not misrepresented any of Professor Whitehead's views. Certainly I must have failed at many points to bring out the subtlety and depth of his ideas. But in spite of the defects of my understanding and presentation, of which I am acutely conscious, I hope the main trends of Professor Whitehead's thought will not be missed by any reader.

Professor A. N. Whitehead is rightly regarded as one of the foremost thinkers of our time. But, unfortunately, as his writings are not always very easy to follow, he is perhaps more admired than read, even by students of philosophy. An age can be said to have rightly appreciated an original thinker only when his ideas are reflected in the modes of its thinking. This, I am afraid, will not be the case with Professor Whitehead until he is more widely read and understood. It is therefore with a view to making his ideas more widely known that I am venturing to publish this book. If anybody is helped in any way by this book in understanding Professor Whitehead's philosophy or in being led to a study of his works, I shall feel my labours have not been in vain. As it is my wish that a reader of this book should ultimately read the works of Professor Whitehead, I have not scrupled to use often his own words to express his ideas, so that the reader may already become familiar with them before he begins to read the original books.

I know Miss Emmet has already published an excellent book on the philosophy of Professor Whitehead. But I believe my treatment will be found somewhat different from hers, and besides I have dealt with certain topics which are not touched in her book. In any case two books certainly cannot be considered too many on so great a philosopher as Professor Whitehead.

R. Das.

Amalner, India.
August 15th, 1937.

CHAPTER I

PHILOSOPHY AND ITS METHOD

" SPECULATIVE PHILOSOPHY ", as defined by Whitehead, " is the endeavour to frame a coherent, logical, necessary system of general ideas in terms of which every element of our experience can be interpreted."[1] We see at once from this definition that philosophy has to do with the intellectual construction of a scheme of ideas which will explain all facts of experience. But what is the meaning of explanation or " interpretation ", as Whitehead calls it ? A fact is interpreted, in the sense intended here, when it is shown as an instance of a general idea. Philosophy explains our experience when it exhibits every item of our experience, that is, everything of which we are conscious, as enjoyed, perceived, willed or thought, as an instance of the general scheme of ideas which it has constructed. Thus the system of ideas has a theoretical and a practical side. It should not merely be entertained in theory but should also be capable of being applied to the facts of experience. On the theoretical side, the system should be coherent and logical. It should be coherent in the sense that it should constitute an interconnected whole, so that no one of its important ideas should be capable of being abstracted from

[1] *Process and Reality*, p. 3.

the rest.   The different ideas in the system should presuppose one another, not in the sense of being definable in terms of one another, but in the sense that each is significant only in relation to the others.   It is presupposed that every entity in the universe is what it is by virtue of its determinate place in the universe, and cannot be conceived to have a being outside this universe. This character of the universe, as reflected in the scheme of ideas, is its coherence.

It should be logical in the sense that the scheme of ideas should be framed in accordance with the logical principle of self-consistency, and general logical notions should be illustrated in it, and also the scheme should provide room for the principles of inference.   It is not meant that logical principles are to be placed above philosophical notions, and are to be regarded as the ultimate first principles.   It is, of course, true that our philosophical ideas should not violate logical principles and should be framed according to them ; but then the logical principles themselves should find their place in the general scheme of philosophical ideas.

On the empirical side, the scheme should be applicable and adequate.   It is applicable if some fact of our experience can be shown as an instance of the general scheme, and the scheme is adequate when it is applicable to every such fact. In other words, all facts which we have experienced and in which we can believe as actual or possible, should be interpretable in terms of the scheme.   It should be universally valid, and in this sense the system of ideas may be regarded as necessary.

It is thus clear that metaphysical principles should be illustrated in all facts of our experience and there should be no facts which can be regarded as exceptions. It might appear that, the metaphysical principles being universal, we could elicit them from a study of any fact. But their very universality is a ground for our not being able to find them out easily. We generally observe by the method of difference. What is found in one place and is not found in another easily attracts our attention. But what is to be found everywhere is apt to be missed by us. Thus we cannot easily discover metaphysical principles, although they are present in all facts. The power of free imagination helps us in our philosophic discovery. In imagination we are not restricted by what we actually see. We may first imaginatively construct ideas, which may afterwards be found present in actual facts. Many mathematical ideas were constructed in this way long before their application to physical reality was suspected. Moreover, we may imagine things which are not actual at all, and thus get the requisite basis of difference for the better observation of actual facts. Thus we see that imagination is a valuable gift for the philosopher. Even the scientist cannot achieve anything of value without this gift. Mere empiricism without imaginative construction leads us nowhere.

But philosophy is not pure imagination. Philosophy requires imagination in the service of knowledge. In all imaginative constructions, such as are necessary in philosophy, we have to be strictly faithful to facts ; we have to see that our imaginative constructions are illustrated in actual facts. Besides, they should satisfy the rational tests of logical consistency and coherence. Empirical verification and logical consistency are the two supreme tests for the sanity of a philosophical scheme. Otherwise it would be indistinguishable from poetry and fiction.

What is said above represents only the ideal which philosophy tries to realize ; but it is not to be supposed that any particular philosophy has realized or is likely to realize this ideal completely. From our present knowledge of the complexity of fact and the weakness of human intelligence, we can only suppose that we may approach the ideal nearer and nearer ; but it is vain to hope that we shall be able to realize the ideal completely. We cannot think of a final metaphysical scheme which will explain all facts completely without leaving anything further to be explained. As we see things at present, there is little likelihood of our attaining a stage when no further progress in philosophic generalization will be necessary or possible. It seems there will be always materials at our disposal to call for better systematization of our metaphysical scheme for enlargement of its scope and increase in its logical rigour. This only means that philosophy, as it is viewed now, is assured of indefinite progress, if only requisite intelligence be forthcoming to carry on its work.

It is clear that Whitehead takes the ordinary method of scientific generalization to be the method of philosophy. It is eminently rational and can be used by ordinary intelligence. One cannot, of course, use the method mechanically and become a great philosopher. No method by itself leads to any such result. We require insight, and that cannot be provided by any method. But what we achieve by our insight should admit of rational presentation and application, and should be intelligible to ordinary understanding. Here Whitehead sets his face against all anti-intellectual intuitionisms which make the possession of some uncommon faculty a necessary qualification for discovering or understanding any philosophical truth.

Thus for Whitehead, philosophy does not represent a peculiar kind of knowledge, having a peculiar field of its own and differing essentially from scientific knowledge in its character and scope. But if the method of philosophy is essentially the method of science, and if philosophic knowledge is not different in character from scientific knowledge, how is, then, philosophy at all different from science? We may readily admit that there is no essential difference in character between philosophic and scientific knowledge. Still, what we learn from philosophy is not what we learn from the sciences. A particular science studies a particular set of facts in abstraction from other facts, which may be related with them but, being of a different kind, do not fall within the scope of this science. Thus science is always limited in scope, and studies facts in abstraction. There is no science which studies all facts, or, at least, aims to arrive at principles that will be applicable to all facts. This work is reserved for philosophy. So the old saying that philosophy is the science of sciences may, in a sense, be true. Two objections may be raised. First, it may be asked, when the facts are studied by the different sciences, what is there left to be studied specially by philosophy? And, secondly, is it possible for anybody to study all facts?

Facts, we have said, are studied by the sciences under limited aspects. Thus the different sciences give us only the partial views of facts, and the partial views themselves cannot constitute the whole view, unless they are properly synthesized and unified. So in order to give us a complete understanding of facts, the work of philosophy is necessary over and above the work of the sciences. The question now comes whether it is possible for any individual to study all the facts which are severally studied by the different sciences. It is obvious that no individual can study all the facts, but it is also true that one does not need to be acquainted with the detailed work of all the sciences in order to become a philosopher. A philosopher may study a few facts in order to arrive at his general conclusions, but these conclusions must be applicable to all facts. The material for philosophy as well as for science is supplied by experience. If the sciences give us reliable knowledge about the facts of experience—and they have no other aim—and if philosophy also is an interpretation of the same facts, then it can ill afford to neglect the evidence of the sciences. It may be difficult to master what the different sciences have to say about the different aspects of reality which they study. But a philosophy which is already familiar with such systematizations of facts as are found in different sciences is likely to do more substantial work than one which ignores the work of the sciences or formulates its principles in defiance of their evidence. Moreover, in philosophy we are concerned with ultimate generalities which are applicable to all facts, and we do not need to know facts in their particular character ; and the ultimate conceptions, which any special science uses, are not many. So, I think, even to-day it is not an impossible task for a philosopher to acquaint himself, as Whitehead has done, with the broad general conceptions of different sciences before he ventures upon any metaphysical constructions.

The method of philosophy, then, is the method of " working hypothesis ". Whitehead calls it also the method of " descriptive generalization ". We tentatively formulate a general metaphysical scheme, and the truth of the scheme depends on the success with which it can be used to interpret the facts of experience. The aim of philosophy is not to give us a peculiar intuition into some transcendental core of reality or to justify our belief in some supersensible entities accepted on faith, but merely to give the most general description of facts.

Whitehead has come to philosophy from mathematics and science, and he has been able to point out certain defects in the methods of modern philosophy. Those of us who have been trained in the tradition of modern European philosophy can hardly think of them as defects. We should think it a good point in a philosopher that he starts with some propositions which are clear and distinct and are absolutely certain. It is sometimes supposed that real knowledge is that which cannot be doubted, and if philosophy is to give us real knowledge, it should start with some indubitable principle, for starting with doubtful premises it can never arrive at indubitable conclusions. Whitehead boldly inverts the whole idea. He says that there are no irreformable, clear and distinct, absolutely certain first principles to start with. Clarity and certainty are gradually to be attained in our knowledge, and they cannot characterize our starting points. This is evident from the method of working hypothesis which, according to Whitehead, philosophy embodies. When we frame a metaphysical hypothesis, we cannot initially be certain about its truth or very clear as to its exact significance. As the hypothetical scheme receives verification in empirical facts, we feel more and more certain about its truth and see more and more clearly its exact significance.

Modern philosophy has also erred, according to Whitehead, in regarding the five senses as the sole gates of our knowledge of the external world, and in relying exclusively upon introspection for the examination of experience. Through the senses we get the knowledge of the contemporary world as illustrated by the sense-data. We know nothing of its past or future, and entirely miss the all-important fact that the present is derived from the past. We should rather regard the whole body as the organ of knowledge. The environment is pressing itself upon the whole body, and through indistinct bodily feelings we become directly aware of the causal derivation of the present from the past. Through the senses we know the world in " presentational immediacy ", and through the bodily feelings we know it in " causal efficacy ". In the former mode, we know the world merely as static, and it is only in the latter mode that we know the world as a causal process.

Introspection similarly gives undue prominence to some aspects of experience, relegating others into the background. The data of sensation are marked clearly, but " the compulsions and derivations which form the main stuff of experience " are not noticed in introspection. " In particular it rules out that intimate sense of derivation from the body, which is the reason for our instinctive identification of our bodies with ourselves."[1] Thus through the senses and in introspection we do not find all our available experiences, and in order to discover the main categories under which the facts of experience can be classified, we should examine experiences of all kinds, whether normal or abnormal, physical or mental.

It is sometimes urged against philosophy that it is a curiously unprogressive branch of knowledge. While the sciences and other branches of knowledge are making rapid progress, we seem to be discussing in philosophy, even to-day, in the same inconclusive manner, the eternal problems which Plato and Aristotle discussed. Whitehead does not share this pessimistic view about philosophy. He thinks that progress is possible and philosophy has actually progressed in the course of history. The different systems of philosophy which have appeared represent no doubt different views of reality, but they are not

[1] *Adventures of Ideas*, p. 290.

to be regarded as absolute alternatives equally
to be condemned for their invalidity. They
rather express " a variety of general truths about
the Universe," and we make progress towards
a final view by co-ordinating and synthesizing
these partial truths. The chief error in philosophy, according to Whitehead, is its overstatement. Every system of philosophy expresses
some truth about reality, and the mistake lies in
regarding this truth as the whole truth. And we
find that the overstatement of one philosophy is
corrected by the counter-statement of another
philosophy. After we have heard a great philosopher, we see even the old problems in a new
light, and we can no longer regard them in the
same old fashion. " Philosophy never reverts ",
says Whitehead, " to its old position after the
shock of a great philosopher."[1]

The main objection against philosophy, however, is that it serves no useful purpose. Those
who urge this objection seem to think, as Bacon
thought, that we should faithfully observe only
particular facts and discover the laws governing
them ; but the broad generalizations and inter-
pretations, with which philosophy concerns itself,
are of no use for this purpose. But unfortunately
there are no bare facts. The facts that we find
are already viewed under the aspects of general
concepts, and are found connected with their
contemporaries and referring to a past and to
a future. This means that the observation of
facts itself is possible in the light of some interpretation and generalization. In this sense
nobody can avoid metaphysics, good or bad.

[1] *Process and Reality*, p. 14.

Philosophy does not initiate interpretation, but tries only to make it systematic.

There can be no arbitrary limit to generalization ; and every science rises to philosophy when it carries its generalizations beyond the limits of its particular sphere. Facts are never fully understood unless their place in the universe is truly seen. This can be done only by a systematic coherent interpretation. As we saw above, the truths of science, viewed absolutely in regard to reality, would be but half-truths. Philosophy serves a very useful purpose when it co-ordinates these half-truths of science and supplies the qualifications under which alone they can be regarded as true.

There has been purely scientific philosophy as well as philosophy with a religious appeal. Whitehead has the great distinction of making philosophy closely associated with both science and religion. He has thereby made philosophy a highly effective and useful activity of the human spirit. Our contact with reality is in the experience of particular facts and in the enjoyment of subjective being. Science arose out of the former and religion out of the latter. The demand for intellectual justification for the brute facts of experience is at the root of science. This demand and the corresponding devotion to truth are fit parallels of religious sentiments. Only in science we are concerned with objective facts and not with subjectivity, which is the concern of religion. In religion we seek to realize, in the particularity of feeling, the general conceptions which can properly be provided by philosophy alone. Religious emotions find their justification in philosophic generalizations, and the philosophic generalizations find their illustration in religious feelings. Both philosophy and religion gain in content and depth by this mutual service. The conceptual scheme provided by philosophy may appear, in its abstract general character, almost valueless ; but it acquires supreme value when it is grasped in the immediacy of a feeling, as we try to do in religion. The tendency towards abstract generalization and the tendency towards emotional realization are both present in the human spirit. They are somewhat opposed in character, dividing science from religion. Unless they are reconciled and fused together, life is sure to suffer from inner deficiency. Merely with science, we get knowledge without value, and with unenlightened religion we get value without truth. But, rational beings that we are, we can be satisfied with neither alone. Philosophy synthesizes science and religion ; and confers value on our knowledge, and reality on our value.

CHAPTER II

SOME PRIMARY IDEAS

THE most fundamental fact about the world is that it is ever moving on. It is never stationary even for a moment. The world at this moment is not what it was a moment ago. Day follows night, and every birth is followed by growth and decay. We can never catch the world taking a holiday from this universal rule of change, growth, process or motion. When we just look at a plant or a chair, we do not apparently find that it is growing or changing. But we know that the plant came out of a seed, and will grow into a tree, not by any big jumps that one can notice. We have therefore to suppose that it is in a continuous process of change. About the chair, too, we know that it is continuously changing, although no change is apparently visible. That everything changes and nothing stands firm, philosophers knew even from ancient times when they did not know anything of modern physics. Modern physics has made it easier to understand perpetual change in nature ; for it has taught us how even the most solid and apparently changeless bodies are nothing but conglomerations of atoms in violent agitation. Thus it is clear that whenever we take anything to be static, it is because we do not think, or see its inner constitution.

Process is universal, and in this process something new is ever coming into being. Novelty is, as it were, the birthright of every creature that is ever born. What comes into being now is not what was there before. Undifferenced persistence of anything actual is not consistent with universal process. The reappearance of the old is possible, only when the old thing has somewhere remained in its self-identity and has thus remained outside the scope of the process. If it is affected by the process, or once ceases to exist, it cannot again be identical with anything that enjoys present existence. The dead can arise, only when they do not actually die.

We have just said that what comes into being is always something new. But the new thing can arise, only when the old has made room for it ; and the old can make room for the new, only by disappearing from the scene. What has now come into being passes out of existence, so that something new may arise in its place. The world dies in order to live. We maintain ourselves only on the basis of our dead selves. Thus if one side of the process is indicated by something new always coming into being, the other side shows something old, or accomplished, always passing out of existence.

Other people besides Whitehead have also believed in universal change, but sometimes this change, which constitutes the character of reality, is conceived as pure change that admits of no intellectual understanding or analysis. It is supposed that we cannot intellectually grasp the character of pure change and that our intellectual analysis always falsifies its real character by turning it into a multiplicity of static bits. The view of change or process here presented is not exactly of this sort. The world-process is not mere process which cannot be further characterized or analysed. The process is not mere going from nowhere to nowhere. It is always accomplishing something, bringing forward something new and dissolving something which is already accomplished.

We have said that what comes into being is something new and it is made possible by the passing out of existence of something that is old. Now the question is whether the new thing that comes into being is altogether new, owing nothing to the old, and whether the old thing, when it dies, dies out completely, bequeathing nothing to the new. If everything were absolutely original, borrowing nothing from the past, then anything might appear anywhere. A tree might grow out of a stone as well as from its proper seed. But we do not find this to be the case. Everything conforms to its own proper conditions.

Moreover, if we had absolute beginning at every moment, there would be no sense of the past. The past is not there to be seen and known by us. Since everything is in the present, if nothing came from what was there before, there would be no occasion to know anything as past. The past has meaning for us, only because we derive our present existence from things that have gone before. The past has died, but not without leaving its sure legacy for the present.

Thus we see that when a thing loses the immediacy of present existence, it is not thereby reduced to mere nothing. It becomes part and parcel of the objective constitution of the world ; and whatever comes into being after it, has to take proper note of it. What has once been in the world leaves its inescapable effect upon the world, and whatever grows out of this world is, to some extent, great or small, determined by the effect.

The present is determined by the past. This determination is nothing else than the conformation of the present to the past, and strict conformation means the reproduction in oneself of the character of that which is conformed to. So if the present were determined solely by the past, there would be little chance of any happening quite novel in character. We have no doubt seen that every event that occurs is new, but it may be new in the sense that, as a unique individual, it is different from all other events that have gone before. But in spite of this numerical difference, it may only reproduce the character of its predecessors. If this were the case, there would be no genuine novelty anywhere. But the emergence of truly novel characters is an undeniable fact. We have therefore to suppose that the present is not determined merely by what has already happened, but also by what has never yet happened and is only sought to be realized by the world process. An event is only a phase in the world process, and it embodies both what has gone before and what the process is coming to. What is past influences the present by way of efficient causality, and what is future operates in the present as the final cause. The process is not an aimless drift. It arises from a settled state of things and proceeds to definite ends. Thus the meanings of efficient and final causality are part of the meaning of the process itself.

Again the process by itself is nothing actual, apart from the things or actualities that come out in the process. It only means that there is no happening by itself apart from what happens. The process is not merely an abortive attempt at accomplishing something. It does in fact result in the production of definite actual entities. These entities are what happen, and they represent the process itself. These entities, appearing and disappearing in causal succession, are the ultimate actualities, the embodiments of the process, beyond which there is nothing.

An actual entity is determined by its predecessors and it also conditions its successors. It is evident that the being of such an entity consists in its being affected by others and in its affecting other actual entities. An actual entity is not anything by itself apart from its relation with other actual entities. The world does not consist of independent self-subsistent entities which can be defined by their private qualities. The entities of the world we know are essentially related to one another and, apart from this essential relation, they are mere fictions. Therefore the notion of substance, implying self-subsistence and possession of private qualities, cannot be applied to them. We cannot, therefore, suppose that actual entities are in their being quite independent of one another and only accidentally enter into relations among themselves. Such an entity, existing in itself and defined by its own private quality or qualities, is never found and cannot be known. We must therefore repudiate the notion of substance as inapplicable in our metaphysics. We must clearly realize that an actual entity has already received in its being contributions from other actual entities, and is there at all only to make its own contribution to the being of other actual entities. This is the principle of relativity to be adopted in the place of the notion of absolute substantiality.

We have just seen that a thing is defined by its relation to other things. What is the nature of this relation ? This relation is nothing but a mode of affection. We may call it a feeling. What I am is clearly shown by how I am affected by other things, i.e. how I feel towards them. The other things enter into my being only through my feeling. If they fail to make themselves felt by me, they are nothing to me. One does not, however, need to be conscious in order to be affected by others. The capacity for being affected by other things is common to all actual beings ; and so we should keep away all suggestion of consciousness from our notion of feeling.

An actual entity is nothing but a unity of feeling in which other entities are grasped. Every actual entity, high or low, is a definite unity of feeling, complex or simple. That which affects, or is affected by, nothing is itself nothing. So the notion of mere matter, of something unfelt and unfeeling, of " vacuous actuality ", must be given up as inapplicable in sound metaphysics. In fact, an actual entity is nothing over and above its feelings. It is how it feels. It can be completely analysed in terms of its feelings. The neutral term " prehension ", a happy coinage of Whitehead, is also used for these feelings, because it brings in no suggestion of higher mentality and can be safely used for atoms and electrons as well as for human beings.

Feelings are the bonds of the universe. It is by means of feelings that many entities, actual and possible, are joined together to form a concrete actual entity. The entity thus formed is, after all, a unity of feeling. The end that guides the formation or growth of the entity is the attainment of the particular unity of feeling realized in the entity. When the end is achieved, the feeling entity lapses into the state of a matter of fact, to be felt by, and thus to be a constituent in, other actual entities. The actual entity unifies its universe by means of its feeling, that is, it holds together in its feeling all those entities which can be felt by it (and which, therefore, constitute its universe).

When the purpose of its being is satisfied, that is, the attainment of the particular unity of feeling is achieved, an actual entity adds itself to other entities as matters of fact. They are all again joined together in a unity of feeling by some other actual entity which in its turn adds itself to their multiplicity when its satisfaction is attained.

The creative process thus works by unifying the many entities, which are already there, into a novel entity, but the new entity does not swallow up the many and annul their multiplicity ; it adds itself to them and increases their multiplicity. " The many become one and are increased by one."[1]

We see how skilfully Whitehead tries here to combine the modern scientific ideas of atomicity and organism in his notion of an actual entity. An actual entity is atomic, because it is a particular, distinct from other entities, and is not really divisible into other actual entities. An actual entity is a unity of feeling and the unity is absolute. It may be a very complex feeling, implying many subordinate feelings as well as objects that are felt. We may analyse them all within the complex unity of the final feeling. But by our analysis we shall not arrive at separate reals which could maintain themselves even outside this unity. But although atomic, an actual entity is also an organism and forms part of other organisms. It is itself a synthesis of many elements, and becomes also an element in other entities. The universe is thus thoroughly organic, and no part of it can be separated from the rest. It does not simply mean that we cannot actually take an entity out of the universe or separate it bodily from among its neighbours. It rather means that the being of an actual entity is defined by its relations to the rest of the universe, and it has no being at all out of those relations.

Philosophy errs gravely when it forgets the universal relatedness of things, and begins to consider anything as real in itself. For purposes of analytical study we may have to make abstractions, but our abstractions are not realities. When we mistake our abstractions for realities,

[1] *Process and Reality*, p. 29.

we commit what Whitehead calls " the fallacy of misplaced concreteness ". Our notions of mere time and mere space are typical instances of this fallacy. The things which are actually real are the concrete actual entities in process of development in intimate relationship with one another. It used to be supposed that space and time were real in themselves in which things and events were to be simply located. That was a mistake. Events or, more strictly, actual occasions are the ultimate realities, and what we call space and time are nothing but certain aspects of these occasions. To regard these aspects as independently real is to commit the above fallacy.

Similarly, the usual view of consciousness as an independent mental fact, divorced from matter or object, is a further instance of this fallacy. Matter and mind are not two independent facts but are two sides of the same fact. An actual entity not only feels but is also felt. As a feeling subject, it may be regarded as mind ; and as felt, it is matter or object. We have discarded the notion of vacuous actuality and cannot believe in the reality of any matter which is not a centre of experience or feeling. But there is no feeling apart from some datum which is felt, and there is no centre of experience which does not itself become a datum for some other experience. Thus there is nothing without a subjective and an objective side. It is therefore erroneous to regard these correlative aspects of fact as completely independent facts.

We are accustomed to regard the events of the world as bifurcated into two series, mental and

physical.   The series of mental events are studied
by psychology, and the series of physical events
are studied by physical science.   For the purposes
of science, such division is inevitable, because
science always works under abstraction.   But
philosophy, which aims at giving a true view of
reality, cannot afford to regard these scientific
abstractions as metaphysical facts.

The last important idea that we want to
explain in this chapter is what Whitehead calls
the ontological principle.   This principle means
that the reason for any fact in the universe is to
be found in one or more actual entities and not
anywhere beyond all actual entities.   They are
the ultimate realities, and the metaphysical
explanation of any facts whatever must be in
terms of actual entities and what is contained as
elements in them.   What is ever adduced as
reason for anything must be capable of being
referred to some actual entity or other.   Every
actual entity physically feels other actual entities
which enter into its constitution and also has
conceptual prehension of (or appetition towards)
what is going to be realized in it.   We may speak
of the latter as its subjective aim.   When we
search for any reason, we in fact search for the
physical feeling or subjective aim of one or more
actual entities.   What is not a fact that is
physically felt or a possible ideal that is conceptually prehended by some actual entity is nothing
at all, and can constitute no metaphysical reason.
Whatever is real must have a foothold in some
actual entity, functioning towards it either as an
efficient cause or as a teleological ideal, and thus
entering into its physical or conceptual feeling.

What does not function either as an efficient cause or as a final cause has no part to play in the creative process and cannot therefore be legitimately introduced in a descriptive account of it which metaphysics seeks to provide.

CHAPTER III

ACTUAL ENTITIES

WE have already learnt something about actual entities. We shall now study their character and constitution in some detail in this chapter.

The most important thing to understand about the nature of an actual entity is that it is not made up of some " stuff ". We referred to this point in the last chapter when we said that an actual entity was not to be conceived as an independent substance. But our ordinary thought is so dominated by the notion of substance that we find it difficult to conceive how an entity can actually exist without being identified with some stuff. But however difficult the conception may be, if we are to understand the nature of an actual entity aright, we must try to conceive it after the manner of a passing process, and not as a standing being. The being of an actual entity is the becoming of a process. When we have repudiated the notion of vacuous actuality, it is best to conceive this process as a process of experience.

Now every experience exhibits the duality of subject and object. If there is to be an experience there must be something to be experienced, and something else which experiences it. Whitehead thus accepts the subject-object structure of experience. But he does not take the subject-object relation to be identical with the relation of knower and known. The relation of knower and known is present only in certain special cases of experience which are possible only for beings with a very high grade of mentality ; but the subject-object relation is present in all cases of experience, and no experience is possible without this relation. The essence of experience is not knowledge, but something else which Whitehead calls feeling. When we have taken reality to be a process of experience, this process should be exemplified in all kinds of existence. But we have no reason to think that knowledge, as clear consciousness of some definite content, is present in sticks and stones, which are not denied existence. We know, however, that every actual being is affected by, has to do with, or is concerned with, other beings. This " having to do with " or " concern " is termed feeling. The red-hot iron feels the fire without knowing it at all.

The subject thus feels the object ; the object is felt, and the subject is the feeler. The feeling subject would ordinarily be conceived as a passive recipient of some influence from the object. Whitehead does not conceive the subject in this way. There is no passive receptivity anywhere. The feeler is itself an active process. If it were to be passively affected by its object, it would require to have already an accomplished being prior to the influence of the object. But that is not the case. The subject, as here conceived, is not already there to be brought under the influence of the object. It comes into being from out of its object, and is, in a sense, thrown up by the latter, and is, therefore, more properly to be called " superject " than subject. The feeler is generated by the object felt and comes on the scene later than the object. One may suppose that the subject must already be there, if there is to be any object, for without a subject there can be no object. Or it may be thought that neither subject nor object enjoys any priority of being and so both must be present together at the same time. In the view presented by Whitehead, both these ideas are rejected. Decided priority is granted to the object from which the subject derives its being. The being of the subject is constituted by its feeling, and there can be no feeling unless the matter to be felt is already there.

By the inherent process of growth, every actual entity is carried beyond itself and produces its own successor. The successor leads to its own successor, and in this way the process of the world goes on. It is thus clear that no actual entity is merely subject or merely object. The terms subject and object are relative. An actual entity is subject in relation to what has gone before it and has conditioned its being. But the same entity assumes the status of an object in relation to its own successor which comes out of it and is conditioned by it.

Every actual entity has thus a dual aspect. It has a formal internal constitution of its own and also an objective constitution which determines other entities. Roughly speaking we may say, it is something for itself and also it is something for others. Viewed in and for itself, it is an act of feeling or a subjective feeler ; and in respect to other entities determined by it, it is an objective matter of fact.

Always it is a question of the growth of some determinate feeling. The world process is not aiming so much at objective results as the production of definite subjective feelings. When the definite subjective unity of feeling, aimed at in a particular process, is attained, the evolving actual entity reaches what is called its " satisfaction " and falls, satisfied and exhausted, into the status of an object. It is then incorporated as an element in the objective constitution of another actual entity which takes its rise from it.

If we imagine the world process as a flow, we find there are two kinds of fluency in it and they are both represented in every actual entity. By one kind of fluency, a subject is developed out of objective data and by the other kind the subject is turned into an object. The first is called " concrescence " and the second is called " transition ". Concrescence means nothing else than the growth of feeling and constitutes the real internal constitution of a particular existence. Transition is the passage from one particular existent to another particular existent by which the former is turned into an object for the latter. Concrescence and transition are not two processes, but are merely two aspects of the same process. If transition is the process of objectification, concrescence is the process of subjectification and neither is possible apart from the other.

An actual entity is not the product of one datum only. We do not have merely linear series in the world, but there are all kinds of intermingling. In fact, all the entities of the actual world, in different degrees of relevance, enter into the constitution of the actual entity which grows out of it. The many entities of the actual world are grasped in a unity of feeling by the actual entity in question, and when it achieves its satisfaction it is itself added as another entity to the many entities of its actual world. The actual worlds of two different actual entities are, however, never exactly alike. The actual world of a particular actual entity is constituted by all those entities which are objectively felt by it, or which enter into its constitution as objective elements. The actual world is thus always defined by the standpoint of some actual entity and is relative to it, and so different with different actual entities.

An actual entity has a definite bond of feeling with each item in its universe. All these feelings are co-ordinated in a final and higher unity of feeling which really defines the internal constitution of the actual entity.

Every actual entity is a particular. But the term particular here should not be understood in the sense that an actual entity does not enter into the description of other actual entities. From the principle of relativity we know that an actual entity always becomes an element in some other entity and so partly defines the character of the latter. When we call an actual entity particular, we merely mean that it has a perfectly definite and determinate being which is distinct from everything else in the universe.

An actual entity is what it is by reason of the various subordinate feelings which are united in it. And these are what they are because of their inclusion in this unity. They are so modified by each other, that they may together form the particular unity which is the resultant actual entity. In the growth of different feelings, derived from different data, there is a control by the subjective aim, which is realized in the final unity of feeling. The creative process aims at the feeler and the feeler determines how it should be constituted. All the constituent feelings get their organization and respective emphasis in the light of the final determinate unity which they are going to constitute. In this sense an actual entity may be said to be its own reason. The form of the final feeling, which integrates all subordinate feelings, as well as the relative importance of these feelings in the final synthesis, is not externally determined. The data to be felt are no doubt supplied by the actual world, but how they should be felt and with what different emphasis, is left completely undetermined. This indetermination is eliminated by the emergence of the actual entity which is a definite unity of feeling. It thus represents the free self-creativity of the universe. It is *causa sui* and is therefore a substance in Spinoza's sense.

The objects to be felt are completely determined. They are given, and are antecedent to the emergent entity which feels them. They may be given less or more importance, but they cannot be altogether ignored. They constitute the stubborn facts of the world from whose influence there is no escape. There is some indetermination with regard to a concrescent feeling till it becomes quite concrete, but the object to be felt is already a concrete thing with a definite character. The object is neither a mode of feeling nor a product of the feeling which prehends it. In the ordinary realistic view, the object is independent of the subject, and there is no necessity that a subject should take cognisance of the object. In Whitehead's view, the object necessarily conditions, and is felt by, the subject.

When an actual entity, after the attainment of its satisfaction, lapses into the status of an object, it remains there as part and parcel of the objective world, to be felt in different degree by all subsequent actual entities. The energy of feeling, after a definite unity in some definite form is reached, falls away exhausted, and the subject it constituted dies away as subject and becomes an object. The creative process moves on by turning the subject into an object. The subject perishes, but in so doing it attains objective immortality. Objective immortality means nothing else than the immortality of the object. When a subject becomes an object, it enters as an objective element into the constitution of some actual entity, and this element is not eliminated even when that actual entity in its turn becomes an object to some other entity. An object thus is repeated in every subsequent entity. It is born, but it never dies.

If A is an object in the actual entity B, and if C and D are actual entities coming after B, then A remains an object for C and D also. It never loses its objectivity or gets dissolved into nothingness. The immortality of the object is the immortality of the past. The past is an unalterable fact, which determines all the future course of history. When a subject loses its subjectivity, the immediacy of present feeling, it is turned into a past fact and it thus attains immortality.

An actual entity is primarily and essentially a subjective unity of feeling. It arises from relevant objects and lapses into the status of an object after its self-fulfilment. But after its birth and before its lapse into objectivity, it enjoys its own decisive moment of absolute reality. It is then in its true nature an absolutely unique individual. It is altogether a novel creation and is never repeated. When it perishes, it is gone for ever. No two actual entities are ever quite alike. They are in a sense absolute particulars. They die but do not change. Change implies persistence through different states; but actual entities are not persisting things.

In virtue of the creative process, dominating the universe, diverse feelings come to be integrated into one feeling, but as soon as the unity or satisfaction is accomplished, the living unity of feeling or the actual entity dies off and is petrified into a matter of fact. An actual entity is therefore more properly called an actual occasion, to get rid of the suggestion of persistence which the term entity may bring in. Only God is never called an actual occasion but always an actual entity.

In spite of the atomic character of actualities, we find continuity in our own life and in nature also. Continuity is explained by the doctrine of conformal feeling. We know that every actual entity conditions its successors. But the successor is not already there to be passively affected by the predecessor. The successor is said to be conditioned by the predecessor because, as it comes into being, it conforms to the latter. And it conforms to its predecessor in the sense that it reproduces in itself the form of feeling which characterizes its predecessor, and thus there appears to be a continuity of feeling. Ultimately there are only occasions of experience. If in the immediate past there is an occasion of experience in which I feel some datum with the form of anger, then in the present also, when the immediate past occasion is a datum of experience, there will be the form of anger in my experience. In the synthesis of many feelings into a full concrete occasion, modifications certainly occur. " But the subjective forms of the immediate past are continuous with those of the present."[1]

We have, I believe, now got some definite idea about an actual entity. It is, after all, an occasion of experience in which the actual world is focused into a unity by bonds of feelings. An occasion is a unity of feeling, comprising many subordinate feelings each having its own proper datum or object.

It is to be noted that consciousness is not an essential factor in an occasion of experience. In the infinitely vast majority of cases, it is not present at all. Consciousness is present only in those occasions of experience in which a very high grade of mentality is involved. But ordinarily an occasion of experience has no implication as to consciousness. Still, if the world is to be understood, it must be understood in the light of our own experience ; and the experience, which we can analyse, is always more or less conscious.

[1] *Adventures of Ideas*, p. 235.

With this proviso, let us try to illustrate the notion of an actual occasion by an instance from our own experience. Whatever else I may be, there is no doubt about the fact that I am an experiencing entity, and my life may be accurately analysed into a series of occasions of experience. My present perception of the world around me may be taken to be one such occasion. The act of perception is a very complicated process which we shall try to explain in a later chapter. For our present purpose we shall ignore all its complexity and view it in a simplified form. We shall also note that what is actually perceived is not merely what emerges in clear consciousness. Many elements fall within our perception which we do not clearly notice ; but, nevertheless, they are really perceived by us, in the sense that in their absence our perception would not be what it is.

If now we regard a perception as an actual occasion, we find that it represents a particular unification of the world from a particular standpoint. I am, at the moment of perception, nothing but the occasion of perceptual experience, and my actual being is defined by what is given in my perception ; and what is actually given is not merely what I clearly see or hear. A certain portion of the spatial world is illuminated by clear consciousness, but beyond it there is always an indefinite horizon which lacks the illumination of clear consciousness and yet influences my perception. In fact, what is clearly seen is not what is given to my perception, considered as an actual occasion. What is really given to this occasion must precede it, but what

is clearly seen is seen as contemporaneous with
this occasion. In any case, there is no difficulty
in understanding the position that whatever
conditions an occasion of perception is an object
in that occasion, and the actual world for any
such occasion is constituted by all those actual
entities which objectively enter into it. My
perception, then, is a feeling unification of the
actual entities of my actual world.

What I should feel is already there and is
absolutely determined, but how I should feel
is not determined. I enjoy free causality with
regard to the form of feeling which defines my
subjective being, and in this sense I am self-made.

Every perception is a definite way of feeling
the world. When a perception is completed,
it becomes a definite datum for the next perception. If it were not so, there would be no
learning by experience. What has once entered
into my experience remains an inescapable fact,
and influences all my subsequent experience. If
a man is bitten by a dog in his childhood, it
continues to influence his behaviour towards dogs
throughout his life, even when he has no memory
of his childhood's experience.

Chapter IV

ETERNAL OBJECTS

THE actual entities, we have seen, are essentially of the nature of passing events, understood in the ordinary sense. An actual entity is an event that happens but once and is never repeated. It enjoys its own decisive moment of self-fulfilment and immediately perishes into the status of a mere datum for some other unit or units of feeling. But although an actual entity, in its concrete particularity, is not found elsewhere and at any other time away from its own place and time of occurrence, it happens under aspects of characters that are everywhere and always the same. An actual entity, in its proper nature, is unique and transitory ; but the characters it exhibits have the same significance everywhere, and may recur at many other places and times. These characters are ordinarily called universals, but Whitehead calls them " eternal objects ". They are the forms of Plato, ideas of Locke and essences of Critical Realists. But Whitehead prefers to use his own term in order that it may remain free from the peculiar associations of the other terms which these philosophers use. The Critical Realists have their own view of essences, which is not exactly the view Whitehead presents about eternal objects. Plato would not recognize as " forms " many of the eternal objects accepted by Whitehead. But a reference to these concepts,

forms and essences, indicates the sort of entities
we have in view when we speak of eternal objects.
Locke speaks of ideas in different senses in
different places ; but at one place he speaks of
some ideas " such as those expressed by the
words whiteness, hardness, sweetness, thinking,
motion, man, elephant, army, drunkenness ",
which will be accepted by Whitehead as eternal
objects. From these parallel ideas, we can easily
get the broad sense of the term eternal object.

Whatever is or happens in the world of existence
appears under some definite forms. It may be
a tree or a storm, but, whatever it is, it has a form
of definiteness by which it is characterized and
may be described. In fact, the world of things
and events is known to us in terms of these forms
or eternal objects. We know the green meadow
and the blue sky, birds and beasts, as well as
ourselves and other men with our joys and
sorrows. Each of these terms, green meadow,
blue sky, bird, beast, man, joy, sorrow, means an
eternal object, inasmuch as it stands for a definite
form which characterizes certain existence.

An existent is a combination of what is
recurrent and what is non-recurrent. An eternal
object represents the recurrent element ; and
since it is available in many actual entities, it is
not essential to its being that it should be present
in any particular actual entity. Whitehead
defines it in this way. " An entity whose
conceptual recognition does not involve a necessary reference to any definite actual entities of the
temporal world is called an ' eternal object.' "[1]
The same thing is expressed by saying that

[1] *Process and Reality*, p. 60.

eternal objects are in their nature abstract. By " abstract " it is meant " that what an eternal object is in itself—that is to say, its essence—is comprehensible without reference to some one particular occasion of experience ".[1] Actual entities are the only things that actually exist, and eternal objects appear in them as representing their definite forms. But, as we have just seen, the meaning and the being of an eternal object are not like those of an actual entity. In contradistinction to *actual* entities, we may speak of eternal objects as merely *possible*. An actual entity is what a thing is, and an eternal object is what a thing may be. We know that a man may be tall or short, fair or dark, wise or foolish. The terms tall, short, etc., meaning different eternal objects, indicate merely the different possibilities for a man. Any one of them in its essence is merely a possible or potential which may or may not be realized in any particular case. When a man is actually short, we have to understand that the possible, short, is realized in his case, but that it still remains a possible for many other persons and things. Even in the case of the short man, shortness was a possibility and therefore he could be short. If it were otherwise, if, that is, shortness were not at all a possibility, he could never be short. In every case of actualization we get a selection out of many possibilities.

Moreover, the meaning of the term short is not strictly confined just to the particular stature which the man in question has. It stands indifferently for a definite kind of stature which

[1] *Science and the Modern World*, p. 228.

many other individuals may as well have. Thus an eternal object is strictly a possibility, and no actuality ever really exhausts its full significance. We therefore say that an eternal object appears or "ingresses" in one or more actual entities, but is not identical with any one of them.

This does not, however, mean that an eternal object ingresses in an actual entity which is already there as a completed being. The ingression of an eternal object in an actual entity means nothing else than the realization of the eternal object by that actual entity. The actual entity comes into being only as an instance of that eternal object, and exists only under that form. It has no existence without being informed by some eternal objects. An actual entity is anything at all, because it is definite, and its definiteness is due to the ingression of eternal objects in it.

An eternal object is a universal in that it is available in many instances ; but it has a particularity of meaning, which is the same in all cases, and is distinct from the meanings of other eternal objects. Every eternal object is thus possessed of a unique individuality. A particular definite shade of red is just that shade of red, which is exactly the same in all cases, wherever it may occur. And it cannot be understood in terms of anything else. We must acquaint ourselves directly with the particular meaning or essence of an eternal object, if we are to understand it at all. An eternal object is the same in different cases in the sense that it has the same significance in all cases. But although an eternal object is identical with itself in every case, the mode of its ingression in different actual entities is different. This we shall understand if we consider the relation of an eternal object to other eternal objects.

We have said that every eternal object has a unique individuality. But this does not mean that eternal objects are not related among themselves or that each of them is distinct through mere lack of relationship with others. On the contrary, the full meaning of an eternal object is brought out by its relations with other eternal objects. We do not find isolated eternal objects unrelated with one another. We find, on the other hand, that certain eternal objects necessarily go with certain other eternal objects, and also exclude certain others. If it is a flower, it is also coloured and soft. Different groups of eternal objects are realized in different actual entities. And if actualization is a selection from the realm of possibilities, then the grouping is determined even in the realm of the possible. In other words, eternal objects, even as abstract possibles, are intimately related among themselves, and some determinately related groups are realized in actual entities. There is no absolutely undetermined possibility. We can never correctly say that *any* thing is possible. The range of possibility may be very wide in a particular case, but it can never be unlimited. Only certain things are possible in a certain case. The eternal objects are the mere possible, and the limitation of the possible is secured by the determinate relationships among the possibles themselves.

The reference to a case cannot be eliminated in considering a possibility. A possible is that which can be actualized. Where there is no question of actualization, there is no meaning of possibility either. So the consideration of the eternal objects cannot be divorced from a general reference to the actual world. Since the constitution of the actual world is quite determined, whatever is possible for it must be also determined. If God gave the first determination to the actual world, He determined at the same time the relationships among the eternal objects which together constitute the total ultimate possibilities for this world. Thus there are interrelated possibilities, which means that the eternal objects are related to one another.

We may even go further and say that the meaning of an eternal object is in a sense determined by its relations to other eternal objects. If we know some eternal objects, and if we also know how a certain other eternal object is related to them, then we can know that other eternal object also. The different shades of a colour, for instance, may be arranged in a series, and so the particular serial relation may be said to hold of the members of the series. Now, if we directly know the immediately earlier and the immediately later member, without directly knowing the intermediate one, then from our knowledge of the earlier and later members and of the particular serial relation, we may very well know the intermediate member also. This is possible because the intermediate member is in a determinate relation with the other members. An eternal object is thus determinately related to all other eternal objects, and it would not be what it is, if its relation to other eternal objects were different. In this sense, it may be said that they are internally related to one another or that each has a relational essence. In other words, the full significance of an eternal object is brought out by its different relations to other eternal objects. Each eternal object is fixed in its determinate relationships to other eternal objects, and cannot be divorced from its determinate place in the realm of eternal objects.

The different relationships of an eternal object may be conceived as different aspects of it, and it may be present in different actual entities in its different aspects. But in one actual entity all the different aspects of an eternal object are not realized, because some of them are contraries. The red in a flower and the red in fire present different aspects of red, and we cannot imagine that both these aspects can be realized in one actual entity.

We have said that a general reference to actuality cannot be eliminated in the consideration of eternal objects. But their relation to actual entities is not determinate like the relation of eternal objects among themselves or like the relation of actual entities to them. The ingression of an eternal object in any particular actual entity is indeterminate in the sense that it is no part of essence of the eternal object to occur or ingress in that particular actual entity. Even if the actual entity in question had not come into being, there would be no loss to the meaning or being of the eternal object. It would still be, as a possible, what it is. There is no indeterminateness, however, as to the relation of the actual entity to the eternal object. The actual entity would not be anything at all without the definiteness of the eternal object which it illustrates. This fact may be expressed technically by saying that the relation of the eternal object to the actual entity is external, and the relation of the actual entity to the eternal object is internal. The eternal object may be well understood without a reference to the actual entity, but the actual entity cannot be conceived apart from the eternal object which is exemplified in it.

Eternal objects may be simple or complex. Several eternal objects in a definite relationship may constitute another eternal object. Such an eternal object is complex. Its complexity means " its analysability into a relationship of component eternal objects". The component eternal objects may also be complex, but ultimately we must come to simple ones. An eternal object is simple, if it cannot be analysed into a relationship of other eternal objects. A definite shade of green may be taken as an instance of a simple eternal object. If we regard humanity as composed of animality and relationality in a particular relationship, then humanity will be a complex eternal object, and its component animality, as expressing a relationship of mind and body, will also be complex.

In any actual entity there will always be a group of simple eternal objects which ingress in that entity in the most concrete fashion. They get identified with the individual essence of the entity. The manner of fusion of the eternal object in an actual entity is quite unique, and cannot be described or explained in terms of anything else. We can only say that in getting fused with one another in an actual entity, the simple eternal objects enter into an infinite variety of relationships with one another, and thus give rise to other eternal objects of higher and higher grades of complexity. There is no end to the complex eternal objects which are constituted out of the simple eternal objects present in an actual entity. All these different complex eternal objects express the different aspects of the actual entity. This brings out the meaning of the familiar statement that there can be no complete description of an actual particular object in terms of concepts. By the term concept we understand an eternal object, and the number of complex eternal objects associated with an actual entity being, as we have just seen, endless, there can be no complete enumeration of them all. This fact is expressed in the Whiteheadian language that there is an infinite abstractive hierarchy associated with an actual entity.

We have spoken of the eternal objects as mere possibles. But what place in reality can a mere possible have ? The actual entities constitute the ultimate stuff of reality. And whatever is real must be one with, or referred to, one or other of these actual entities. A mere possible apart from a place in some actual entity is indistinguishable from nonentity. Our notion of an eternal object is not, however, that of a nonentity. The eternal objects must therefore be referred to some actual entity.

An actual entity consists of its feelings. The feelings of an actual entity as well as the actual

entity itself are actual, whereas the eternal
objects are merely possible and not actual. And
we can feel what is possible as well as what is
actual. Our hopes and fears always refer to
what may be, but is not yet actual. So when
the eternal objects are referred to some actual
entity, we have to understand that they are
referred as objects of some feeling entertained
by that entity.

When the object felt is an actual entity, the
feeling is called physical ; and when the object
is an eternal object, the feeling is called conceptual. In order to save them from the fate of
nothingness, the eternal objects are referred to
the conceptual feeling of God. As entertained
in that feeling, they are real and get related with
one another. God envisages the whole range of
eternal objects with all their determinate relationships. God's conceptual realization determines
what they are and how they are related. As
present in the mind of God, they constitute a sort
of Platonic world of ideas. It should not be
supposed that God creates the eternal objects.
They are necessary to His being as He is to them.
God is God because He has the conceptual
feeling of all the eternal objects ; and the
eternal objects are anything at all, and can
function in an actual entity, only because they
are entertained in God's conceptual feeling.

The ultimate possibilities envisaged by God
gradually become actual in the creative process.
What is present in the mind of God comes
within the grasp of the created actual entities also.
This grasp or prehension may be of two kinds,
positive and negative. An actual entity is

determined not only by what it includes but also by what it excludes. It is determined, that is, by what it negatively prehends as well as by what it positively prehends. Understanding prehension in the general sense of relation, we can see how a term is determined by its negative as well as by its positive relations. We get real information about a horse when we learn that it is not an ass. The bareness of a mountain, i.e. the absence of trees and herbs on it, is also a character of it. Thus we can understand how a negative prehension expresses a positive bond. Every eternal object has thus some relevance in the determination of an actual entity, as it must be felt either positively or negatively. Only we have to recognize that the relevance of every eternal object is not equally important. It may be in many cases very slight and quite negligible. If by the term " feeling " we understand only positive prehensions, then we have to say that only a selection of eternal objects are felt by any given actual entity.

We have spoken of eternal objects as forms of definiteness, and so we should understand that, when they ingress in an actual entity, their function is to render definite some aspects of the actual entity. Now an actual entity consists of a feeling and what is felt. What is felt may be an actuality or a possibility. Thus an eternal object, when it ingresses in an actual entity, defines the form of (1) a feeling or (2) an actuality or (3) a possibility, that is felt. These are the three modes of ingression of an eternal object in an actual entity.

In the third mode, the eternal object appears as

a mere possibility, which is capable of realization
in either of the other two modes. " It is a real
ingression into actuality, but it is a restricted
ingression ",[1] because the eternal object is prehended as a mere possible and there is no
immediate realization of its function as a definite
form.

In the first two modes, there is unrestricted
ingression of eternal object. But the two modes
are not indifferently open to all eternal objects.
The eternal objects may be classified as subjective
or objective, according as they obtain ingression
in the first mode or the second mode. The forms
of feeling are subjective and the forms of felt
are objective. Ordinarily an objective form is
not also a subjective form, and vice versa. An
object seen (felt) may be defined as chair, but no
feeling will ever be defined as chair. Love is
a form of subjective feeling, and is never a form
of objective being. The sense-data, however,
define the feelings and also what is felt. Whitehead says we have a red feeling towards an
object which is also recognized as red.

An eternal object, merely as a possible, is
properly an object of conceptual feeling. The
form of such a feeling is valuation, positive or
negative. That is to say, there is always an
appetition towards, or a repulsion from, a
possibility.

---

[1] *Process and Reality*, p. 412.

CHAPTER V

GROUPS AND GRADES OF ACTUAL ENTITIES

WE have seen that the actual entities are the ultimate realities in the universe. But the things of the universe, given in our unsophisticated knowledge, do not appear in the form of actual entities, as described in the foregoing pages. There are stars and planets in the sky, as well as birds, beasts, and men on earth. There are space and time, and matter, organic and inorganic. We must be naturally curious to know how these are to be understood in terms of actual entities, and if they, mountains and stars, birds and beasts, are not themselves actual entities, we should like to know how they are constituted out of actual entities, since actual entities are the ultimate metaphysical facts.

In order to be able to give an account of these things in terms of actual entities, we must first understand how the actual entities are related among themselves. Whitehead speaks of his philosophy as the philosophy of organism. From this we get the clear hint that the actual entities are in organic connection with one another. They are, as it were, the parts of an organism. It is the characteristic of an organism that its parts determine each other. They are in a sense immanent in each other. This mutual immanence or universal relativity is a very important point in Whitehead's philosophy. We have already seen how the actual entities of the past are present in the constitution of those of the present. We will now try to see how the future is immanent in the present and how the contemporary actual entities are present in one another.

It sounds rather paradoxical that the future should be immanent in the present. The future is not yet, and it is difficult to conceive how what is not yet should still be present. But in that way one may not also allow even the past to be immanent in the present. The past is what is gone, and how can what is gone be present also ? So we should understand in what sense the past or the future is immanent in the present. The past is immanent in the present, not in the sense that the past is not past, but only in the sense that it objectively determines the present. The past has exercised its efficient causality with regard to the present and has allowed itself to be inherited by the present actual occasion as part of its objective constitution.

The future cannot of course be immanent in the present in this sense. The past actual entities were actual facts which could have their causal influence on the present. The future, however, does not represent any determinate actual entities, and cannot therefore, like the past, influence the present. But at the same time we cannot say that the future is nothing, or altogether indifferent to the present. If we look to the distant future, we may not clearly see how there is any effective connection between the present and the future. But if we consider the immediate future, which is ahead of the present by less than one-tenth of a second, we at once see that it is in a way already made in the present. What is just going to be is very largely what now is. The present being what it is, the future has to be of a determinate character in conformity with the present. There is continuous becoming, and the future issues out of the present. In the onrush of creative advance, the future is precipitated out of the womb of the present, and it bears in itself the marks and traces of its origin. This only means that the present is pregnant with the future, and that the shape of the future can be discerned, however dimly, already in the present. There is an inherent necessity in the present that there should be a future, and a future of a definite character.

Since there are no gaps in the creative becoming, every actual occasion is effectively connected both with what goes before it and what comes after it. It looks before and after. We should know that the occasion arises as an effect facing its past and ends as a cause facing its future.[1] As effect it re-enacts the past and as cause it anticipates the future. The immediate past is re-enacted in the present. And the future is immanent in the present in anticipation.

The individual future occasions are not existent now, but still the future has an objective existence in the present. The present is definite and it has a definite future. The definiteness of the future is determined by the definite present. " The future is immanent in the present by reason of the fact that the present bears in its own essence

[1] *Adventures of Ideas*, p. 249.

the relationships which it will have to the future. It thereby includes in its essence the necessities to which the future must conform."[1]

It might be supposed that if the future is already immanent in the present, then nothing new ever comes into being. But this would be a mistake. The novelty of creation is a keynote of Whitehead's philosophy. In many cases no doubt the past is merely repeated, and the new element is quite negligible. This is so in very low grades of actualities. But creation does not present us in every case with monotonous repetition. In a new synthesis, in most cases, much is eliminated as well as added, so that the emergent actuality is not in every detail like its predecessor. The past lays down conditions which have certainly to be conformed to, but it always leaves room enough for the exercise of free creativity. The past cannot be ignored and has to be felt under all conditions, but how it is to be felt and with what different emphasis on its different elements remains undecided till the emergence of the new actual entity.

Although the immanence of the future in the present is not like that of the past, it is yet quite direct. But when we come to consider the contemporary actual entities, we find that they have no direct connection at all. The relation of past and future is a causal relation. A thing can be in the past or future of another only when there is a causal connection between them. The absolute view of time, which conceives the past or future of a thing without any regard to the causal or physical connection between them, is

[1] *Adventures of Ideas*, p. 250.

given up here. A thing is in my past only when I am causally determined by it, and, similarly, a thing is in my future when I can determine it causally. From this point of view, my contemporaries are causally independent of me. They cannot be causally connected with me without falling in my past or future, i.e. without ceasing to be my contemporaries. Causal independence is thus the meaning of contemporariness.

How are the contemporary occasions then immanent in each other? Although two such occasions are causally independent, they yet have a common past and a common future. They are immanent in the common past (in the way the future is immanent in the present), and the common past is immanent, and enjoys its objective immortality, in them both. Thus through their common past, they are immanent in each other. Similarly, through their common future, they are mutually connected. We say that the contemporary occasions are indirectly immanent in each other, because there is no direct connection between them except through their past or future.

It may be noted that according to the notion of time, here adopted, the contemporaries of contemporaries need not themselves be contemporaries. If X is causally independent (i.e. a contemporary) of Y, and Y is causally independent of Z, then X and Z may or may not be causally independent of each other.

We must try to understand another notion before we can tackle the main question of this chapter. That notion is the notion of order. The data that are felt, when considered in themselves, exhibit neither order nor disorder. They are merely given and are what they are. We find order or disorder in them when we view them in the light of some ideal which they fulfil or fail to fulfil. Thus the consideration of some end gives meaning to the notion of order. There is order in the actual world in so far as its different elements are adapted for the attainment of an end. When the question of adaptation to an end is not raised, we find mere givenness, and order has no meaning.

What is the end that the things in the world can subserve ? The only function assigned to them is that of entering as objective data into the feeling of some actual entity. And an actual entity aims at a satisfaction or a completed unity of feeling. So the end, which the things in the world can subserve, is some degree of intensity in the satisfaction of actual entities. Intensity of feeling is the end of creative advance. There is thus order in the actual world when its different elements contribute to some intensity of feeling. Feeling is heightened by contrast. It is a commonplace of psychology that things appear striking by contrast. This only means that contrast contributes to the intensity of our feeling. But if certain things are so unlike each other that they are really incompatible, then instead of heightening the feeling, they will destroy the unity of feeling. In fact they cannot together explicitly enter into any feeling. Thus the actual world or a group of actual entities will exhibit order when its many different elements enter explicitly into a feeling as contrasts and are not required to be ignored as incompatibilities.

We have said that intensity of feeling is the end or ideal which gives meaning to order. But there is no one ideal which determines the order or disorder of all actual entities. There are different ideals for different groups of actual entities according to their grades, and these ideals determine different kinds of order. What is order in a particular group of one sort may be disorder in another group of a different sort. What is order in the earth particles in a lump of clay is not order in the group of living cells composing a human body. The orders are different, because the ideals to be subserved in the two cases are different.

Again, the ideal in a particular case may be only partially fulfilled ; so there may be partial order as well as disorder. We have only to remember that order promotes the intensity of satisfaction, whereas disorder enfeebles it.

The notion of order as explained above applies primarily to the objectified data for individual actual entities. The data are orderly when the resultant feeling, which transcends the data, is of a particular degree of intensity. But we also speak of order in nature, as also in a man's life. In such cases we take order to be a certain relationship among a group of actual entities. When we speak of order in nature, we take nature to be a group of actual entities and order stands for a relationship which is enjoyed by them. In the case of a man's life, too, we take it to be a group of actual occasions, and a particular relationship of these is the order in the man's life. In both these cases, order is not understood by reference to a transcendent ideal, but stands for a relationship of actual entities themselves.

It is a relationship of actual entities among themselves, in virtue of which they form a society. Order in this sense is important for our present purpose, as it introduces the correlative notion of a " society ". The term society is here used in a technical sense and stands for an " ordered " group of actual entities. And so the meaning of order will come out when we try to understand the characteristics of a society in the technical sense.

At the outset it is probably well to distinguish the notion of a society from that of a nexus. A nexus is a group of actual entities which enjoys the very general relation of mutual immanence explained before. A nexus does not presuppose anything more than this general metaphysical relation of mutual immanence on the part of its members. A nexus can have both temporal and spatial extensions. If it is purely spatial, it includes only such actual entities as are contemporary with each other ; and if it is purely temporal, there are then no contemporary actual entities in it, but only those that are relatively past and future.

A society is also a nexus, but a nexus of a special type. A nexus of actual entities is called a society when its members exhibit a common form and when the common form, found in a member, is due to the effect of other members upon it. The common form is the defining character of the society. The important point is that the members of a society must be alike in some respect and their likeness must be due to their being born in that society. A member of a society owes its similarity to other members to its genetic derivation from them. The common form, defining a society and found in each one of its members, is inherited from member to member. There is no society where there is no social inheritance or tradition.

The sort of relationship just explained, in virtue of which the members of a nexus constitute a society, is called social order. Briefly, therefore, we may say, " A society is a nexus which illustrates or ' shares in ' some type of ' social order.' "[1]

Whitehead gives a rather unusual instance of a society. The life of a man may be conceived as an historic route of actual occasions. Now a group of such occasions, dating, say, from the man's learning of the Greek language up to his loss of any adequate knowledge of the same, constitutes a society, because its different members, i.e. the different actual occasions, exhibit a common characteristic, viz. knowledge of Greek, and this characteristic is inherited from occasion to occasion. Knowledge of Greek is the defining character of this society. Ordinarily, however, we employ a more important characteristic to define a society.

Although the term society has been defined here for technical use, it very well satisfies our ordinary notion of a society. Where there is a society, there must be some common characteristics possessed by the different individuals constituting that society, and a person possesses those common characteristics solely because he is born in that society.

[1] *Adventures of Ideas*, p. 261.

From the above description, it is quite clear that there cannot be a society of merely contemporary members. Contemporary actual entities are never conceived in genetic relation with one another and so there can be no genetic inheritance between them. They may well be, however, included in a society which includes their successors and predecessors. Thus a society must possess the quality of endurance. " The real actual things that endure are all societies."[1] But though it has a history, it has no identity of actual being. Its identity is that of its defining character only. It is quite unlike actual entities which have no history, because they come into being and die away and do not endure. Unless a society is wholly in the past, we cannot have a definite completed nexus of actual entities constituting a society, because in a living society new members are constantly being added.

Another fact to be noted about a society is that it is not found in isolation. It has always a background of wider environment to the laws of which the members of the society are subject, in addition to the laws of their own society.

We have said that all real actual things that endure are societies. We may even say the universe we live in is a hierarchy of societies in which the narrower ones are parts, and further specializations, of the wider ones. If the Indians form a society, the Indian Hindus are a sub-society, such that they are part of the wider Indian society, and, besides possessing the common characters of Indians, possess their special character of being Hindus. The Indian society

[1] *Adventures of Ideas*, p. 262.

forms the background of the Hindu society. The members of the Hindu society have to obey the common laws of the Indian society and have, besides, to follow the special laws of their own society. An animal body is a society which is possible only in the wider environment of so-called material bodies. And the parts of an animal body have to follow the more general laws of material bodies, and have, besides, their own special laws. Thus we can understand " the principle that every society requires a social background, of which it is itself a part ".[1]

As the background becomes wider and wider, its defining character, too, becomes more and more general. The ultimate society, that may be supposed to lie at the farthest background of our present epoch, is bound together by such a most general relationship that it scarcely appears to be a definite connection at all. Whitehead says that " from the standpoint of our present epoch, the fundamental society in so far as it transcends our own epoch seems a vast confusion mitigated by the few faint elements of order contained in its own defining characteristic of ' extensive connection.' "[2] Within this society we have the geometrical society of pure extension. Pure extension is more specialized than extensive connection, as we shall see later. Within the geometrical society, we have the still more specialized society of electro-magnetic occasions. This electro-magnetic society dominates our present epoch or the so-called physical universe in which we are living. It " exhibits the

[1] *Process and Reality*, p. 125.
[2] Ibid., p. 135.

physical electro-magnetic field which is the topic
of physical science ".[1]

The electro-magnetic society provides the
background for other specialized societies in
which are realized the peculiar intensities of
experience which are not realizable in the mere
electro-magnetic society. " The physical world
exhibits a bewildering complexity of such societies,
favouring each other, competing with each other.
The most general examples of such societies are
the regular trains of waves, individual electrons,
protons, individual molecules, societies of molecules such as inorganic bodies, living cells, and
societies of cells such as vegetables and animal
bodies."[2]

We have said that all enduring objects are
societies. But to understand their proper nature,
we must introduce the notion of " personal
order ". We know that a society is a nexus that
enjoys social order. And personal order is a
special kind of social order, so that personal order
can be found only in a society. A society enjoys
personal order when the genetic relation of its
members orders them serially. In an ordinary
society, in which there are contemporary members as well as past and future ones, the members
cannot strictly be ordered serially in virtue of
their genetic relation. All the members of such
a society cannot be arranged in a line according
to their birth. One member arises out of many,
and there are others between which there is no
direct genetic relation. But a nexus, which is
purely temporal (in the sense explained above)

[1] *Process and Reality*, p. 137.
[2] Ibid., p. 137.

and continuous, admits of serial arrangement in virtue of the genetic relation of its members. Such a nexus is a society which is a person. This is also the conception of an enduring object. " A society may be analysable into many strands of enduring objects." At least this is so in the case of most ordinary objects.

We raised the question, at the beginning of this chapter : How are mountains and stars, trees and animals, to be conceived in terms of actual entities ? We can give some answer to this question now. That which persists through time is a nexus of temporal occasions. In actual reality one single self-identical atom does not run through a length of time, but there is only a continuous succession of atomic occasions which constitute a society. Thus what we call an atom is nothing but a society of atomic occasions. And since these exhibit an identical form due to their genetic derivation, and can be serially arranged, the atom is to be regarded as an enduring object. A mountain or a star can also be viewed in the same way. They consist, however, of innumerable strands of enduring objects. They are indeed very complex societies, having societies within societies in them. Even an atom is a complex society, having electronic and protonic societies within it. Our chairs and tables, vegetable and animal bodies represent, as it were, subordinate universes containing innumerable subordinate enduring objects.[1] What we call nature is itself " a complex of enduring objects ".

But there is some obvious difference between

[1] *Adventures of Ideas*, p. 265.

a stone and a tree or an animal.   The difference
is constituted by the presence of life in the latter
bodies.   How is life to be understood ?

We know that an actual occasion feels its
datum and thus takes it up into its own constitution, but it feels the datum in its own way and
thus makes its own contribution to the final
satisfaction.   Novelty is introduced by the new
feeling of the resulting occasion.   There is no
actual occasion which entirely fails to make this
novel contribution.   But in many cases the
novel contribution is so very insignificant that it
may be said to be non-existent, so that the new
occasion may be supposed to be merely repeating
what it has received.   This is the case with all
non-living actual entities.   We know what we
call a stone is really a succession of stony occasions,
and in this succession we get mere repetitions
without any appreciable novel addition.   The
stony occasion now is scarcely to be distinguished
from what has just gone before it, the novel
addition is so very insignificant.   In ordinary
language we may say that chairs and tables
continue of themselves in the same state, and
therein lies their lifelessness.   But the case with
a tree, or any other living body, is different.
Each of the actual occasions, which constitute
its life, makes its own novel contribution.   A
living thing is growing every moment, and does
not continue in the same state.   If it remained in
the same state, it would be indistinguishable
from a non-living thing.   A living thing adapts
itself to its changing environments by novel
reactions to them, and is not thus bound absolutely by them.   Adaptation, novel reaction or

freedom means originality. Where there is no originativeness, there is no life.

There is, however, no absolute gap between the living and the non-living. Every actual occasion is a new creation and there is some novelty in every creation. There is life only where novelty or originality is distinctive. We know that every actual occasion is bipolar, having a mental as well as a physical pole. In every occasion something of the past is repeated, and there is also something new. The physical pole accounts for what is repeated and the mental pole for what is new. There is life where the mental pole predominates. To put the matter in another form, we may say there is life where the facts are not explicable by efficient causality alone. The phenomena of life are exactly those which cannot be explained merely by the efficient or physical causes, for they explain what is repeated and not what is original.

A vegetable or animal body is a " living society ". A living society does not require that all its constituent occasions should be living. It is enough if some of them are living. " Thus a society may be more or less living according to the prevalence in it of living occasions."[1] In a structured society, various nexūs[2] are co-ordinated in a systematic way, and some of them are regnant, and some are subservient. Some of these may be entirely living and some not so. Usually a society is called living when the regnant nexūs in it are entirely living. A living society involves nexūs which are inorganic

[1] *Process and Reality*, p. 143.
[2] Plural of nexus.

or non-living. " We do not know of any living society devoid of its subservient apparatus of inorganic societies."[1]

In fact the entirely living nexūs, apart from the animal body, do not properly form a society at all. A society requires a defining character, which is inherited from occasion to occasion. But life cannot be a defining character, because it is not inherited, but comes out in novel reaction. " It is the name for originality, and not for tradition."[2]

Another important characteristic of life is that it necessitates consumption of food. A non-living society does not need to destroy any other society in its environment ; but a living society does destroy other elaborate societies derived from its environment, in order to maintain itself. The societies so destroyed are its food. But why is food needed at all to maintain life ? In order to answer this question, we have to understand where life resides and how it reacts on its physical basis. We know that life means originality and that it does not simply reiterate what is handed down from the past. We also know that by physical causation we get only reiteration, and if physical causation is confined to physical matter or occupied space, then we may conjecture " that life is a characteristic of ' empty space.' " Whitehead says, " Life lurks in the interstices of each living cell, and in the interstices of the brain."[3] A living cell is a highly complex structure of inorganic societies, and in its empty space, where life is taken to reside, chemical associations and dissociations take place, which would not otherwise occur. Thus the stability

[1] *Process and Reality*, p. 144.   [2] Ibid., p. 146.   [3] Ibid., p. 147.

of the structure is constantly being disturbed, and requires to be kept up by the absorption of appropriate complex societies from outside. These are its food. " Thus life acts as though it were a catalytic agent."[1]

We have seen that a living nexus is not a society ; still it may support a thread of personal order along some historical route of its members. Such an enduring entity will be a living person. It is quite evident that life has no essential connection with consciousness. It has also no essential connection with personality. Personality requires a serial personal order of living occasions. In the case of vegetables and lower animals, we have no reason to suspect living personality. Higher animals, in whom we find some central direction, are very probably endowed with living personality. In our self-consciousness, we become directly aware of our own personality.

We should not suppose that there is one life pervading or informing a living body. All the life in the body is the life of individual cells. The living body is a co-ordination of innumerable living actual occasions. In a higher organism, various grades of occasions are so co-ordinated that in some occasions there is a peculiar intensity of experience on account of their inheritance from other occasions. " Finally, the brain is co-ordinated so that a peculiar richness of inheritance is enjoyed now by this and now by that part ; and thus there is produced the presiding personality at that moment in the body."[2]

[1] *Process and Reality*, p. 148.
[2] Ibid., p. 152.

A person feels differently at different times and in different moods. This is accounted for by the fact that different regions of the brain support the presiding occasion at different times. If, in spite of this difference, there is the sense of the same personality, it is because there is an inheritance of character from presiding occasion to presiding occasion. This inheritance makes personal order possible, and gives rise to a single personality ; where this fails, we have either many personalities or no personality at all.

Our soul, then, is an enduring object formed by inheritance from presiding occasion to presiding occasion. " This route of presiding occasions probably wanders ", says Whitehead, " from part to part of the brain, dissociated from the physical material atoms."[1]   But will this route, which constitutes our soul, come to nothing when the brain is disintegrated by death ? Whitehead says that the everlasting nature of God may establish a peculiarly intense relationship of mutual immanence with the soul, so that " in some important sense the existence of the soul may be freed from its complete dependence upon the bodily organization ".[2]

The above account of the various groups and grades of actual entities is, as Whitehead admits, largely conjectural. The special characteristics assigned to various complex entities do not follow from any metaphysical principles. They are not, however, inconsistent with his cosmological doctrines.

On the whole, Whitehead has distinguished

[1] *Process and Reality*, p. 153.
[2] *Adventures of Ideas*, p. 267.

four grades of actual occasions, though they are not sharply to be divided from one another. Space, matter, life, and consciousness describe four main types of existence, and Whitehead's four grades of actual occasions correspond to these. He writes : " First, and lowest, there are the actual occasions in so-called ' empty space ' ; secondly, there are the actual occasions which are moments in the life-histories of enduring non-living objects, such as electrons or other primitive organisms ; thirdly, there are the actual occasions which are moments in the life-histories of enduring living objects; fourthly, there are the actual occasions which are moments in the life-histories of enduring objects with conscious knowledge.''[1]

[1] *Process and Reality*, p. 250.

Chapter VI

THE EXTENSIVE CONTINUUM

THE actual world, as it is given to our perceptual experience, is extended in space and time. But when we say that the world is extended in space and time, we do not mean that space and time are real independent entities which contain the extended world. Space and time are nothing else than the spatio-temporal extension of the world. Spatio-temporality is a mode of extension, and is not itself the meaning of extension. The primary fact is that the world is extended, and this extension has assumed the spatio-temporal form in our present actual world.

Let us first try to understand the character of the world as extended. It is best conceived as an extensive continuum. It is an infinite extension with no gap or break anywhere. We know whatever has been, is, or will be, actual, must find its place in this extensive world. Nothing can claim to be actual if it cannot be put somewhere in the extensive world.

But is the extensive continuum itself actual or is it merely potential ? And how is it exactly to be conceived ? The extended world, as we see it, appears to be quite passive ; and if activity is essential to everything actual, then we may say that the extended world is not actual. But the passive appearance of the extended world is due to the conditions of perception, and not to the lack of activity on the part of the entities which compose the world. In perception we have knowledge of contemporary objects, and contemporaneity is defined as causal independence ; and so the perceived entities do not appear in their causal or active aspects, otherwise they would not be contemporaries of the percipient. But though merely from its passive appearance we cannot rightly say that the extended world is not actual, when we consider its aspect of continuity we can hardly resist this conclusion. Continuity means divisibility but not actual division. And we know that actual entities are all separated from one another. They are divided, and are atomic in character. Although we say that all actual entities must find their place in the extended world, we cannot suppose that they ever lose their individuality and actually form a continuous whole. When we objectify the actual world as continuous extension, the actual entities composing this world are not objectified in their separate, individual, atomic character. In all objectification, there is some abstraction or elimination. When we see a table, we do not see all its actual properties. We objectify or view it only under some limited aspects. A green field of grass is seen as a continuous green sheet from a distance, but actually one green blade is separated from another, and there is much non-green space between them. Similarly, when the world is seen as a continuous extension, it is objectified only in its very general aspect of extensity which is capable of division but is not divided. The continuous extended world is thus only potential

and not actual.   Its extensity is itself a kind of
potentiality.

We may distinguish two kinds of potentiality.
There is first " the general potentiality, which is
the bundle of possibilities, mutually consistent
or alternative, provided by the multiplicity of
eternal objects ".[1]   We have already seen that
an eternal object is only a possible.   Certain
eternal objects are incompatible with each other,
and so they are not possible together.   Certain
others are consistent with each other and they
may occur together.   But whatever happens
must illustrate some eternal objects.   All the
possibilities are thus in a sense determined by the
multiplicity of eternal objects.   But they represent a most general kind of possibility.   We do
not know either when, or whether at all, any
group of eternal objects is going to be actual.
In themselves they are mere possibles.   In
distinction from this potentiality, we have the
" real " potentiality which is conditioned by the
data provided by the actual world.   The present
actual world determines what is going to be in
future.   There is always a creative advance
beyond the given actual data, but the advance
is always in conformity with the data.   Anything
and everything allowed by the consistent combination of eternal objects is not going to happen
in the future of any actual world, but only those
things which conform to the present actual data.
The actual world thus determines a possibility
which is more limited than the possibility
permitted by the multiplicity of eternal objects.
This possibility is the real possibility, while

[1] *Process and Reality*, p. 90.

the other is a possibility of the most general kind.

The actual world is a relative thing. It never means the same thing for two different actual entities. The actual world is always understood in reference to some actual entity. All those actual entities, which are objectified by, or enter into the objective constitution of, some other actual entity, constitute the actual world of that actual entity. Thus the actual world is always defined from some standpoint, i.e. from the standpoint of some actual entity. So we find that while the general potentiality is absolute, the real potentiality is relative to some actual entity, from whose standpoint the actual world is defined.

The real potentiality is no doubt relative to a standpoint, so that it varies with different standpoints ; still " the real potentialities relative to all standpoints are co-ordinated as diverse determinations of one extensive continuum ".[1] The extensive continuum is a generalized form of all real potentialities from all standpoints. Whatever is to be actual must occur in it. " This extensive continuum is one relational complex in which all potential objectifications find their niche. It underlies the whole world, past, present, and future."[2] The extensive continuum or extension is a scheme of relationships in which everything must enter in order to be actual.

As the extensive continuum is a general form of real potentiality, we can easily understand that it is not to be conceived as a pre-existent

[1] *Process and Reality*, p. 91.   [2] Ibid., p. 91.

structure, real before the birth of the world. It is the first determination of order arising out of the general character of the world. Real potentiality indicates the sort of things that are possible on account of the nature of the actual world. When the world, i.e. a group of actual entities, is once precipitated into existence, the character of all actual entities really possible is also thereby determined. There are more and more specific determinations, but the first and most general determination is that all actual entities must share relationships which characterize the extensive continuum. Apart from spatialization and temporalization the extensive continuum does not involve shapes, dimensions or measurability. It involves merely the primary relationships of whole to part, of overlapping, of contact, and other relationships derived from these.

We have seen that the real potentiality is understood in reference to some actual world, and the actual world is defined from some standpoint, and so the real potentiality is always relative to a standpoint. When the real potentialities from all standpoints are co-ordinated, we have the generalized idea of the extensive continuum. Thus it appears that the extensive continuum is an ideal construct ; but it is not on that account unreal. It is real, because it expresses a fact derived from the actual world. It expresses those general conditions which are satisfied by all actual entities, past, present and future. Whatever is to be actual must be extensively related. All other specific relationships are possible on the basis of this general relationship.

Many philosophers have maintained—and we can easily understand the statement—that whatever exists must exist somewhere (in space) and at some time. To be in space and time is to be a member of a relational complex. We have to generalize the notions of space and time to get an idea of the extensive continuum. It is more primitive and more general than the space-time of our physical world. Instead of saying that an actual entity must be somewhere in space-time, which is true only of our present cosmic epoch, we say more generally that an actual entity must find its place in the extensive continuum. Our space and time are specific determinations of the extensive continuum. Our space has three dimensions, and if we follow the modern notion, we have to conceive space-time as four-dimensional; but mere extension may have any dimensions or no dimension at all. And also the seriality of time cannot be derived from the notion of mere extension. " The extensiveness of space is really the spatialization of extension ; and the extensiveness of time is really the temporalization of extension."[1]

We have seen that extension is the most general scheme of real potentiality. In actuality, the potential scheme is atomized and divided. This atomization is effected by actual entities. An actual entity is the enjoyment of a certain quantum of time and has a spatial volume. Thus, instead of a continuously running time, we have only temporal jumps. We have, as it were, all at once a stretch of time, and then another, and so on. What actually is there is

[1] *Process and Reality*, p. 409.

the process of becoming which is the becoming of actual entities with their temporal stretch and spatial volume. There is no other process of mere time, over and above this actual process of becoming. And in this process we have, as it were, slabs of time, one followed by another. These slabs may be called epochal durations, the word " epoch " being understood in its Greek sense of arrest.

These durations are extended and so have parts. But these parts are never realized independently. A whole duration does not become real as a result of its parts becoming real one after another. This would mean that the whole presupposed the parts. But here in fact the parts presuppose the whole. As in the case of an actual entity, constituted by several feelings, a constituent feeling is determined by the whole it is going, along with others, to constitute, so in the case of an epochal duration, its parts are what they are only as elements in that whole and are not separately and independently real. " The epochal duration is not realized *via* its *successive* divisible parts, but is given *with* its parts."[1] What are successively real are these whole durations, and succession in this sense is not carried within the durations themselves. This is what is meant by the epochal theory of time. The essence of this theory is that time is not a continuous process but an atomic succession; what we call time is nothing but a succession of definite quanta of time, determined by the nature of the actual entities which enjoy them, and ultimately by the subjective aims which are

[1] *Science and the Modern World*, p. 183.

realized in those actual entities. This means that time does not flow uniformly, but moves, as it were, by jumps, and that a duration of time, although infinitely divisible, is nevertheless completely given.

The conception of space-time here envisaged will be perhaps better understood by contrasting it with the Newtonian conception of time and space. Newton believed in absolute time and absolute space, apart from all relations with sensible objects. In distinction from the absolute mathematical time and space, he referred to the relative time and space conceived by the vulgar in relation to sensible objects. Whitehead favours the view of the vulgar and refines their idea of sensible object into his notion of actual entity. All the time and space, which are real, are, according to him, what is embodied in actual entities. For Newton, absolute durations of time and absolute places were actual things. They were real by themselves. For Whitehead, space and time represent mere abstract aspects of actual things, and are not real by themselves, but are only potential. It is in this sense that Whitehead says that Newton confuses real potentiality with actual fact.

Following the Newtonian notion, we are accustomed to think that things and events occupy space and time which are distinct from them. But in fact there is no space or time apart from the actual entities which are the ultimate actual facts in the universe. The actual entities are spatial and temporal ; they embody in themselves space and time, and do not require a further space or time in which to exist. If we still say that what is to be actual must exist in time and space, we mean merely that it must enter into a special scheme of extensive relationships, which in the end is the meaning of space and time. Space and time are thus a kind of relationship, and not receptacles in which things and èvents are to be housed as foreign contents. Instead of having two kinds of entities, one (things and events) existing in another (space and time), we have a single kind of things (actual occasions) existing in themselves. In the place of uniformly running continuous extensions, space and time, we have only atomized quanta of spatio-temporal extension.

The spatio-temporal occasions are the substitutes for Newton's absolute places and durations. Newton denied motion and change of his absolute places and durations. The order of the parts of time is immutable ; what is earlier cannot become later. The parts of space, too, are fixed as regards their position and so they cannot move. The material things could be supposed to move, i.e. change their place, because they were conceived as distinct from their place. But portions of space are identical with their place, and so they cannot change their place without changing themselves. If they were to move, they would have to be moved out of themselves, which is absurd.

In the same way we find that change and, therefore, motion, have to be denied of actual occasions. The individuality of an actual occasion is absolutely determined by its spatio-temporal relations. In a different spatio-temporal relationship, we have a different actual occasion.

Roughly speaking, we can say that the same actual occasion cannot be found at different places and times. The actual occasions arise and perish, but do not change. If they could remain the same at different places and times, we could then significantly speak of their undergoing change. But since they are identified with their space-time, that is with some definite spatio-temporal relationship, a change of this relationship means a change of the terms themselves. When the relationship ceases, the terms also disappear.

Ordinarily, it is supposed that spatial and temporal relations are external. Mere space and time, it is said, have no influence on the nature of actual things. This view is directly repudiated by the present theory of spatio-temporality as inherent in actual occasions. It means that spatio-temporal relations are internal. The actual occasions in one set of spatio-temporal relations altogether cease to exist when the particular relationship they sustain ceases. There are no actual occasions which could indifferently be in this or that spatio-temporal relationship with no prejudice to their substantial being.

How should we then understand change and motion which we still continue to ascribe to things of the world? To understand change or motion, we must introduce here the technical idea of " event ". In its technical sense an event is not understood as a happening or an actual occasion. " An event is a nexus of actual occasions inter-related in some determinate fashion in some extensive quantum."[1] " For example, a molecule is a historic route of actual

[1] *Process and Reality*, p. 111.

occasions ; and such a route is an ' event.' "[1]
An event is thus a group of actual occasions so
related to one another as to constitute one
extensive quantum. A molecule as an event is
a spatial volume elongated in time, consisting
ultimately of molecular occasions, inter-related
in a particular way.

" The most general sense of the meaning of
change is ' the difference between actual occasions in one event.' "[2] When in common par-
lance we say that a thing has changed, we mean
that it has remained the same and has also
become different. But how is this possible ?
Sameness seems opposed to difference. Whitehead solves this problem by ascribing difference
to actual occasions and identity to the whole
group which is an event ; and so for him identity
and difference do not conflict with each other,
because they are not asserted of one and the
same thing. We can thus significantly speak of
change only in connection with actual occasions
which are different and yet form part of a single
event.

Motion is understood in the same way. The
motion of a molecule, for instance, is " nothing
else than the differences between the successive
occasions of its life-history in respect to the
extensive quanta from which they arise ".[3]
In the case of motion, too, we have to take into
consideration the difference between two successive occasions within a single event, but the
difference is understood only in respect to the
extensive quanta from which the occasions arise.
In simpler language, motion means difference

[1] *Process and Reality*, p. 112.   [2] Ibid., p. 112.   [3] Ibid., p. 112.

between successive occasions in respect to their spatio-temporal relations. Change or motion thus does not belong to any actual occasion by itself, and is after all a kind of relation between actual occasions comprised in an event.

We have seen in this chapter that the extensive continuum is the first determination of real potentiality. It is a general scheme of relationships in which everything actual, whether past, present or future, must enter. The scheme in itself is abstract and only potential. It is actualized in actual entities. Every actual entity in its relationships to other actual entities illustrates this scheme and is, in this sense, somewhere in the extensive continuum. But in another sense an actual entity includes the continuum, because its objective constitution includes the actual world as objectified, and thereby includes the continuum.

All actualities are prehended only as in this continuum. Roughly speaking, we can prehend anything only as extended, and arising from a past and tending to a future. Thus the extensive continuum is a form of intuition, just as space and time are forms of intuition to Kant. But it is not a pure form in Kant's sense, because it is derived from the actual world as datum. For Kant the forms of intuition are productive of the ordered world ; for Whitehead the form of intuition (the extensive continuum) is derivative from the world which is already ordered in itself.

The actual world has extension and the standpoint from which it is defined is also extended. Thus the actual entities experienced and the experiencing unit are all united by their extensive relationships, " in the solidarity of one common world ". Whatever comes into being is extensive and amounts to a quantum.

But is " becoming " or coming into being itself extensive ? Whitehead answers this question in the negative. Only when an actual occasion has become concrete, it exhibits extensive relationships ; but its becoming concrete or concrescence is not extensive and is not therefore in physical time. Time is objective ; subjectivity is beyond time.

Chapter VII

PROPOSITIONS

WHAT is felt in a pure physical feeling is an actual entity ; what is felt in a pure conceptual feeling is an eternal object or a mere possibility. A conceptual feeling is impure when it is integrated with a physical feeling. " The datum of an impure prehension is a proposition, otherwise termed a ' theory.' "[1] A proposition is thus neither an actuality nor a mere possibility, but a possibility restricted to a certain range of actuality. Let us explain.

We know that every actuality is a selection out of many possibilities. When one thing happens, there are many other things which might also happen. The battle of Waterloo resulted in the defeat of Napoleon, and there followed certain changes in our actual world. But Napoleon might have won the battle also. In that case the ensuing changes in the actual world would have been different from what they were. Now the changes which could have happened but did not actually happen are possibilities. But they are not indeterminate or mere possibilities, without any relation to actual fact ; they are, on the contrary, possibilities of a definite kind, relevant to the facts which actually happened. There are always many possibilities or eternal objects (abstract notions expressing the possibilities)

[1] *Process and Reality*, p. 260.

relevant to a particular actual fact. " Thus, in
our actual world of to-day, there is a penumbra
of eternal objects, constituted by relevance to
the Battle of Waterloo."[1]   About any actual fact,
there is a penumbra of eternal objects, expressing
the alternative courses which the events may take,
although only one such course is realized in fact.
The eternal objects or possibilities here are
a limited group, being strictly determined by
their relevance to the actual fact in question.
An element in this penumbral complex is what is
called a proposition.   It is a new kind of entity,
intermediate between actual entities and eternal
objects.   In fact it is a hybrid between them.
A proposition is not absolutely general like an
eternal object, nor absolutely particular like an
actual entity.   A group of generalities relevant,
and so restricted, to a particular range of actual
entities, constitutes a propositional complex, of
which propositions are elements.   In a proposition we have the generalization of a nexus of
particulars to a relevant group of various
possibilities, and the restriction of a group of
universals to a united field of particulars.

A proposition thus involves a set of actual
entities and a set of eternal objects.   The eternal
objects are the possibilities for the actual entities.
Without the basis of some actual entities, we
cannot think of any definite real possibilities.
" The definite set of actual entities involved are
called the ' logical subjects of the proposition ' ;
and the definite set of eternal objects involved
are called the ' predicates of the proposition.' "[2]

[1] *Process and Reality*, p. 262.
[2] Ibid., p. 263.

The predicates define what is possible for the subjects.

The actual entities required to serve as the logical subjects of a proposition can be provided only by the actual world, and the actual world requires an actual occasion from whose standpoint it is defined. The logical subjects of a proposition must always fall within the actual worlds of some actual occasions. These actual occasions constitute the locus of the proposition. " The ' locus ' of a proposition consists of those actual occasions whose actual worlds include the logical subjects of the proposition."[1]

We have already seen that a proposition is felt in an impure conceptual feeling, that is, in a conceptual feeling which is integrated with a physical feeling. Unless a proposition is felt, it cannot be said to be realized at all. A proposition is felt and realized only by a member of its locus.

In propositional feelings, the physical feelings of the actual entities, which are the logical subjects, are integrated with the conceptual feelings of the eternal objects which are the predicates. And the physical feelings of the actual entities are possible only for those actual occasions in whose actual worlds the actual entities fall. The locus of a proposition thus consists of those actual occasions into whose feelings it can enter and by which alone it can be realized.

Ordinarily a proposition is taken to be a judgment or the verbal expression of a judgment. It is what we know of something, and our

[1] *Process and Reality*, p. 263.

knowledge may be expressed in the form of a verbal assertion. In the view we are explaining here, a proposition, in the first place, is no subjective knowledge but an objective entity, and has nothing to do with verbal expression. In fact, language is never adequate to the expression of a proposition. In Whitehead's words, " a verbal statement is never the full expression of a proposition ".[1] Secondly, a proposition is not primarily known, but merely entertained in feeling, and feeling need not be conscious. Most of the propositions never rise up to the level of consciousness.

This view of propositions seems akin to the view according to which propositions subsist like universals, and hold good even when they are not known. The two views are similar in that propositions are regarded as objective entities which need not be known. But there is a difference also. In Whitehead's view, although a proposition is somewhat of a universal, it involves some particulars or actual entities. In the other view, a proposition does not involve any particular actual entity. It further regards a proposition as real by itself, but for Whitehead a proposition is realized only in the feeling of some actual entity. Apart from such realization, a proposition is only " a manner of germaneness of a certain set of eternal objects to a certain set of actual entities ".[2]

There are four main types of entities in the universe. The two primary types are actual entities and eternal objects, and the two hybrid

[1] *Process and Reality*, p. 272.
[2] Ibid., p. 266.

types are feelings and propositions. Feelings are real components of actual entities ; and propositions are only realizable in certain feelings which prehend them as their data or objects.

From the above it is clear that a proposition has primarily to do with a group of actual entities together with a definite set of eternal objects that express the possibilities which are open, or relevant, to the actual entities, and the subject and the predicate of the proposition are selected respectively from these groups. " Socrates is a fool " is a proposition, in which the term " Socrates " stands for a particular group of actual entities and " fool " expresses a possibility for this group. Socrates was not in fact a fool, but as he was a man he might have been a fool. So the eternal object " fool " is relevant to Socrates in a way in which it is not relevant to my pen, because, although we may arbitrarily say " the pen is a fool ", nobody ever feels or views the pen in that light.

This leads to the fact, already explained, that a proposition presupposes some actual entities into whose feelings it can enter as a datum, and by whom it can be realized. This follows from the fact that the actual entities which are to serve as the logical subjects of a proposition must be in the actual worlds of some other actual entities. The proposition can be felt and realized only by these actual entities. The above proposition, " Socrates is a fool ", cannot be realized by persons who lived before Socrates, because the society of actual occasions, for which the term Socrates stands, did not belong to their actual worlds and was not real for them. We can realize this proposition, because for us Socrates is a settled fact and forms part of our actual world.

We may note in this connection that the logical subjects of a proposition do not constitute the entire actual worlds of those by whom the proposition is felt. The actual world in every case includes a wide background, but no sharp distinction is made in general between the background and the actual entities which are the logical subjects of the proposition. When in reflective consciousness we assert a proposition, we no doubt try to distinguish the logical subjects from other elements in the actual world. But propositions are not entertained always in consciousness, far less in reflective consciousness. They are in most cases merely felt, and in such feeling the logical subjects are felt as shading off into a wide and indefinite background.

This brings us to the question of the main function of a proposition. A proposition, according to Whitehead, is not so much for knowing as for feeling. When a propositional feeling develops into consciousness, the proposition may be known, but it is not at all necessary that a propositional feeling should be conscious. Everything in the universe subserves the growth of some feeling, and a proposition is no exception to this rule. In fact the primary function of a proposition is to elicit some novel feeling. Actual entities no doubt contribute to our physical feelings, but some novelty is surely introduced in our feelings when the actual entities are felt, not merely as they are, but as they may be, that is, with their potentialities. Potentiality transcends actuality, and when realized in feeling it introduces novelty which mere actuality cannot provide. Mere physical feelings of actual entities are apt to be repetitive. A proposition effectively subserves the production of new feelings, by including in itself elements of potentiality (eternal objects) which go beyond actuality.

We are constantly feeling actual entities in a propositional way, that is, along with their relevant eternal objects ; but we rarely make explicit judgments. A proposition thus enters our experience primarily to elicit novel feelings but only secondarily to be judged as true or false. Whitehead illustrates this point by referring to the speech of Hamlet which begins with " To be or not to be ". Nobody who reads this speech begins by judging whether the initial proposition is true or false. The speech is meant solely to contribute to our aesthetic enjoyment. Similar is the case with all propositions.

We have already seen that a proposition is neither identical with a judgment nor an expression of it. We now see that it is not primarily judged. But at some stage of mental growth, judgment does appear, and when it appears we find proposition involved in judgment. A judgment is a feeling and it appears in the process or growth of the judging subject. A proposition is included in the objective datum that is felt in a judgment. Broadly speaking, we may say that a judgment is a feeling and a proposition is felt, remembering that what is felt in a judgment is always something more than a proposition. A proposition is the datum of a propositional feeling. A judgment is the synthesis of two feelings, one of which is propositional and the other physical. The physical feeling of an objectified nexus is integrated with the conceptual feeling of a proposition, and this results in the intellectual prehension of the conformity or non-conformity between the nexus and the proposition. This intellectual prehension is what we call a judgment.

A judgment is an actual feeling and expresses a real fact in the constitution of the judging subject. Primarily a judgment expresses a state of the judging actual entity, as inclusive of the feeling and what is felt. The actual entities which are the logical subjects, must be in the actual world of the judging subject, and the actual world is the same thing as its objective constitution. The judgment thus affirms a real fact in the constitution of the judging subject. Ultimately therefore, the judgment is made by the judging subject about itself. But explicitly it is concerned with the actual entities which are the logical subjects of the proposition. It affirms these entities also. There is thus a twofold affirmation in a judgment. But the affirmation about the logical subjects is to be distinguished from the affirmation about the judging subject. In one case a real fact in the constitution of the judging subject is affirmed, and in the other, some eternal objects, qualities, relations, are affirmed of the logical subjects. Evidently the meaning of affirmation is not the same in the two cases. " This affirmation about the logical subjects is obviously ' affirmation ' in a sense derivative from the meaning of ' affirmation ' about the judging subject."[1]

[1] *Process and Reality*, p. 271.

We have seen that every proposition presupposes some definite actual entities which are to be its logical subjects, and these are settled facts in the actual worlds of the judging subjects. The proposition is non-existent for those actual entities whose actual worlds do not contain the settled facts presupposed by it. Besides the requisite constitution of the actual world, a judgment presupposes knowledge of the actual entities presupposed by the proposition. The judgment is not possible for those who lack this requisite knowledge.

It is obvious that we cannot speak of truth or falsehood indifferently about a judgment as well as about a proposition in the same sense. According to Whitehead, a judgment can be correct, incorrect or suspended, whereas only a proposition can be true or false. The judgment is concerned with the conformity or non-conformity of two components within one experience, the objectified nexus and the proposition, both being included in the experience of the judging subject. According as they are coherent or incoherent, the judgment is correct or incorrect. The truth or falsehood of a proposition, however, is determined by the relation of the proposition and the objectified nexus, without restriction to any individual experience in which they may or may not be felt. It is determined by the real character of the nexus and the proposition independently of any individual experience. Whitehead thus supports a correspondence theory of truth and falsehood of propositions and a coherence theory of correctness and incorrectness of judgments.

From what we have said above, it must be

evident that the logical subjects of a proposition are what we would ordinarily call particulars. The particulars must be indicated, because the proposition concerns just these and no others. Without indication, there would be no determinate particulars, and without determinate particulars there would be no propositions, because they must have their logical subjects. It may be thought that a particular can be indicated, or pointed out, as a " this " by a judging subject. But if this were the only way of arriving at determinate particulars, then no proposition would be possible about facts which are not directly felt by a judging subject. Whitehead believes that the particular subject of experience can be eliminated from the fact experienced, and that actual entities in their particularity can be determined by their systematic relation with other actual entities. There is thus an indicative relational system which suffices to determine, from the standpoint of any of its terms, the particularity of its other terms. " Every proposition presupposes some general nexus with an indicative relational system. This nexus includes its locus of judging subjects and also its logical subjects."[1] Propositions are possible only on the basis of such a nexus with a systematic connection. Propositions are not possible in a world where no term is determined by its systematic relations with other terms. This makes clear how the actual world, in some systematic aspect, enters into every proposition, that is, in determining its logical subjects.

We are now brought to the last question of this

[1] *Process and Reality*, p. 276.

chapter. If prepositions are concerned with particular logical subjects, and if they presuppose a definite systematic constitution of the actual world, then are there any metaphysical propositions possible, which must be universally true and not merely of a particular actual world? Even if they are possible, do we know any metaphysical proposition?

Now, although a proposition must be about particular logical subjects, it does not mean that its truth should be confined to those subjects only. A metaphysical proposition is that which can be asserted of any actual entity. Every actual entity possesses certain general properties which can be found everywhere. The very possibility of metaphysics depends on this fact. So we can view particular facts in their most general aspects, and thus try to arrive at metaphysical propositions. But although metaphysical propositions are quite possible, it is difficult to say whether even the most general propositions we know are truly metaphysical, whether, that is, they would be true everywhere and always and not merely in our present cosmic epoch. Even the theorem " one and one make two " may not be universally true ; for it is possible to conceive that, under certain circumstances, two entities may coalesce into one, in which case it would not be true to say that one and one make two.

CHAPTER VIII

FEELINGS

WHITEHEAD calls his philosophy the philosophy of organism. He presents an organic view of reality, and the organizing principle is feeling. It will not be inappropriate to call his philosophy the philosophy of feeling. If we could still speak of stuff—a notion which is discarded by Whitehead—we might say that feeling was the very stuff of reality. Feeling constitutes not only the cement but also the bricks of the philosophic edifice which Whitehead has reared. The actual entities are not only related with one another through feeling, but they themselves are nothing but unities of feeling. What does not feel or has not entered into any feeling is not real at all. If anything is to be real, it must be a factor in some feeling either as subject or as object. A study of feelings, therefore, is supremely important for a full understanding of Whitehead's philosophy. We already know something about feeling as it is understood here. We shall now study, in this and the next chapter, the various kinds of feelings, and also the rules of their combination.

It may be well to remind ourselves here that actual entities are the ultimate things in the world. They appropriate for the foundation of their existence the various elements of the universe, out of which they arise. " Each process of appropriation of a particular element is termed a prehension. The ultimate elements of the universe, thus appropriated, are the already constituted actual entities, and the eternal objects."[1] The universe is always one, because all the actual entities in it enter into the positive prehension of, and are thus unified by, some one actual entity, from the standpoint of which the universe is viewed. There is no viewing the world except from the standpoint of some actual entity.

An actual entity is essentially a process with a subjective unity, but in the course of the process many operations, with incomplete subjective unity, take place, and they terminate in a completed unity, which is called satisfaction. The many subordinate operations are dominated by the subjective unity of the whole process, and they are what the inner life of the actual entity consists of. The living process is continued so long as it has not attained the completed subjective unity or its satisfaction. When the stage of satisfaction is reached, the process drops down exhausted into a matter of fact to enter, as a datum, into the life-process of some other actual entity.

An actual entity is itself a major operation with many subordinate operations directed to, or rather aiming at, the same end. So an actual entity is a complex unity of feelings with many subordinate feelings. By a feeling we understand nothing but a positive prehension.

When feelings enter into a living process, there is growth from feeling to feeling, and one feeling

[1] *Process and Reality*, p. 309.

gets integrated with another till all together constitute the complex unity which is the actual entity itself.   To study the feelings, their growth, and integration, is to study the real internal constitution of the actual entity which they constitute.   It is to study the actual entity as it is in itself, and not as it is for some other actual entity.   This study, which may be called formal and genetic, may be contrasted with the objective or morphological study, which considers the actual entity as a matter of fact, as it functions as a datum in the constitution of some other actual entity.   In the present study, we have to consider the factors involved in a feeling and its different kinds, as also the way in which different feelings grow from, and are integrated with, one another.

A feeling is " essentially a transition effecting a concrescence ".   It involves five factors.   " The factors are :—(i) the ' subject ' which feels, (ii) the ' initial data ' which are to be felt, (iii) the ' elimination ' in virtue of negative prehensions, (iv) the ' objective datum ' which is felt, (v) the ' subjective form ' which is how that subject feels that objective datum."[1]

Let us see what these factors really mean.   We can easily understand that there can be no feeling without a feeler, that is, an entity which entertains the feeling.   This is called the subject.   A feeling cannot be abstracted from its subject. But ordinarily we think that the subject must already be there and a feeling simply supervenes upon it, and we take the subject to be the basis of feeling.   In Whitehead's conception, the

[1] *Process and Reality*, p. 312.

process does not start from the subject, but the subject is, as it were, thrown up by the process. So he prefers the term superject to subject. The subject-superject is the end at which the feelings aim. Strange as it may sound, in Whitehead's view the feelings aim at the feeler. Feelings originate with the sole aim that there may come into being some definite actual entity which will include them into a unity. We are not, however, to suppose that there are first feelings and only then there arises a subject to appropriate them. The subject, after all, is a concrete unity of feelings, and this unity is also the end at which the feelings aim. But the feelings cannot be separated from their end. It is not that any feeling can enter into any unity. The particular unity, into which a feeling is going to enter, is already marked in, or conformed to, by the feeling in question. " The feelings are what they are in order that their subject may be what it is."[1] The subject is what it is because of its feelings. If we look upon the subject as the final cause of the feelings, we may say that the final cause is already inherent in the effect. An actual entity thus may be said to be its own cause.

The initial data are the entities which are to be felt. There is a distinction between the initial datum and the objective datum. The initial datum is no doubt what is felt, but it is felt under one or other of its aspects. It is not felt in its nakedness, with all that is really ingredient in it. When we see a chair, we do not actually see all that there is in the chair. We make abstractions, and always view it under some one aspect.

[1] *Process and Reality*, p. 313.

Similarly, when the initial datum is felt it is felt in some of its aspects, while its other aspects are ignored, or, as it is technically expressed, eliminated by negative prehensions.   The objective datum is what the initial datum is felt as. The objective datum is therefore described as the perspective of the initial datum.   There is progress from the second factor (initial datum) to the fourth (objective datum) through the operation of the third factor (elimination).

We now come to the last factor, the subjective form.   The subjective form expresses how the objective datum is felt by the subject.   It is really the character or form of the feeling as immanent in the feeling.   When, for instance, we see or touch something (i.e. feel an actuality), we may be pleased or displeased ; or again, when we conceive some idea (eternal object), we may tend to realize it or turn away from it. The qualities of joy or distaste, adversion or aversion, are the subjective forms of our feelings. The subjective form is wholly immanent in the feeling in contrast with the datum and the subject-superject which are partly transcendent. The datum enters the feeling, but has also a being prior to the feeling, from which in fact the feeling originates.   The subject-superject has its being in the feeling, but is also something beyond the feeling.   The subjective form as such has no being apart from the feeling, and exists wholly in it.   These facts are expressed in medieval terminology in the following way.   " In the analysis of a feeling, whatever presents itself as also *ante rem* is a datum, whatever presents itself exclusively *in re* is subjective form, whatever presents itself *in re* and *post rem* is ' subject-superject.' "[1]

Feelings are classified according to the nature of their data. The datum may be (i) an actual entity, or (ii) a group of actualities, i.e. a nexus, or (iii) an eternal object by itself or (iv) as associated with some actual entities, i.e. a proposition. We never have a group of eternal objects constituting another eternal object, although there are complex eternal objects. Correspondingly we have four broad classes of feelings : (i) simple physical feelings, (ii) transmuted feelings, (iii) conceptual feelings, and (iv) propositional feelings. Physical feelings and conceptual feelings are the primary feelings, and all the more complex feelings are developed out of these.

The datum of a simple physical feeling is an actual entity, and a nexus of actual entities is the datum of a transmuted feeling. Thus simple physical feelings and transmuted feelings constitute the class of physical feelings. An eternal object is the datum of a conceptual feeling, and a proposition is the datum of a propositional feeling. In both these kinds of feelings some eternal object is the datum. Only in a conceptual feeling the eternal object is taken as a mere possible, without any restriction or definition as to the range of its application. The eternal object in a conceptual feeling has no reference to any actuality. But in a propositional feeling, the eternal object is taken as a possible in reference to a restricted area of actuality. It is still a possible only, but in reference to a limited range of actual entities.

[1] *Process and Reality*, p. 329.

The simple physical feelings are of two kinds, pure and hybrid. In all cases of physical feelings, the initial datum is an actual entity, but the initial datum may be objectified by one of its own physical feelings or by one of its conceptual feelings. That is to say, the objective datum may be a physical feeling, or a conceptual feeling, entertained by the initial datum. If the objective datum of a simple physical feeling is another physical feeling, entertained by the actual entity, which is the initial datum, then the simple physical feeling in question is pure. If the objective datum is a conceptual feeling as felt by the initial datum, then the simple physical feeling is hybrid. In other words, a simple physical feeling is pure when it feels another physical feeling entertained by the initial datum, and it is hybrid when it feels a conceptual feeling entertained by the initial datum.

An actual entity in itself is a feeling subject. It is what it is by virtue of its feelings, and it counts for others only by its feelings. And it is only by means of its feelings that it conditions the creative process which goes on beyond itself. Therefore, when the initial datum is an actual entity, as in the case of all simple physical feelings, it has necessarily to be objectified by one or other of its own feelings. When it is objectified by a physical feeling of its own, it gives rise to a simple physical feeling which is pure ; and when it is objectified by one of its conceptual feelings, we have a simple physical feeling which is hybrid.

But what, after all, is the nature of a simple physical feeling ? Whitehead says that it is an act of causation. " The actual entity which is the initial datum is the ' cause ', the simple physical feeling is the ' effect.' "[1] The subject entertaining the simple physical feeling is in fact only " conditioned " by the effect ; but it is also called the effect.

A simple physical feeling can also be regarded as an act of perception of the most primitive type in which no consciousness is involved. The initial datum is what is perceived and the objective datum is the perspective under which the initial datum is perceived, and the subject entertaining the simple physical feeling is the perceiver.

The subjective form of a simple physical feeling is the subjective form of the feeling which is felt by it. It is variously described as " re-enaction ", " reproduction ", and " conformation ". The subject conforms to the datum, which is to be physically felt, by re-enacting or reproducing the feeling of the datum.

We can thus see how the cause passes into the effect. When the feeling of the initial datum or the cause is reproduced in the effect, the cause, too, comes to be present in the effect, because the reproduced feeling cannot be separated from its subject, the cause. It is in this way that the past is being gathered up into the present. " Simple physical feelings embody the reproductive character of nature, and also the objective immortality of the past."[2]

We may try to understand such feelings by taking a comparatively simple instance. What is ordinarily described as the passage of an electron

[1] *Process and Reality*, p. 334.   [2] Ibid., p. 336.

through space, may be regarded, in terms of this philosophy, as a series of electronic occasions. Each occasion is an actual entity which is the effect of the one that immediately precedes it. The later occasion is said to feel the earlier one physically, and in doing so, it reproduces the feeling of the earlier occasion and thus repeats it. There is thus an incessant flow of feeling from occasion to occasion which leads to ever new creations, but in creating the new, it also preserves the old.

If the physical feelings were everything, the past would be simply repeated, and nothing really new would ever arise. Each occasion would be still new in the sense that it was never before, but, although new in this sense, it would be exactly like its predecessors. The emergence of genuine novelty is provided for by the doctrine of conceptual feelings.

The world at any moment is, no doubt, very largely what it was at the previous moment, but at the same time there is some deviation from its previous state. This means that the actualities composing the world do not simply repeat the actual, as they would do by mere physical feelings, but they realize also new possibilities. But then nothing can be realized unless it is entertained in feeling. The possible is not an actuality that can be physically felt. We can feel it only conceptually. What is meant by a conceptual feeling is a sense of, or an appetition towards, a new possibility. It is a sense of not being bound down by the determined past, an experience of incipient freedom. We all have this feeling. Even an electronic occasion, although dominated almost wholly by the past, is not altogether devoid of this dim appetition towards some unactualized possibility. This is how there is room for novelty even in the inorganic world.

The subjective form of a conceptual feeling has the character of " valuation ". To say how we feel an eternal object is to say what " value " or importance the object has in our feeling. If the eternal object is highly interesting, it is felt as important, and there is a greater urge towards its realization. Or it may be felt as of little importance, and we become indifferent towards it. Thus there may be " valuation up " or " valuation down ", determining what importance an eternal object is to have in the integration and evolution of feelings.

We can easily see how valuation is proper only to conceptual feelings. When we physically feel an actual entity, we are completely under the weight of a dead fact which has simply to be admitted. There is no room for valuation ; we have perforce merely to reproduce the object physically felt. Valuation is proper to an ideal which is not an inescapable fact, but a possibility that may or may not be actualized. According as it is felt or valued, it plays its role in synthesizing or evolving other feelings.

How does a conceptual feeling arise ? How do we get an eternal object that can be conceptually felt ? Conceptual feelings are primarily derived from physical feelings. All the eternal objects are realized in the conceptual feeling of God.

Since God is an actual entity, we can feel Him only physically, but we can feel Him as entertaining a conceptual feeling, and thus an eternal

object will be part of the datum of our feeling.
Thus through a hybrid physical feeling of God,
an eternal object may enter our feeling.   Eternal
objects are also illustrated in the definiteness of
the actual entities already constituted.   So from
a feeling of these actual entities also, we may
derive a feeling of the eternal object which is
illustrated in them.   But we cannot properly
understand the derivation and integration of
feelings unless we understand the principles
according to which such derivation and integration take place.   Whitehead calls these principles
Categoreal Obligations.

The first is the category of subjective unity.
We have seen that an actual entity in its growth
passes through many phases till it reaches the
stage of satisfaction.   These phases are constituted by feelings with incomplete subjective
unity.   Many feelings thus enter into the constitution of an actual entity.   But they are not
integrated when they are in an incomplete
phase.   They get fully integrated when the final
stage is reached.   But by their nature they must
be capable of being integrated or unified in the
final stage.   The feelings in an incomplete phase,
just as they arise, are, as it were, meant for one
another to be members of a common brotherhood.
They all aim at one subjective unity, and the
unity is of the component feelings.   Their
common end already operates in the birth and
growth of the feelings, and in being conditioned
by the common aim they are conditioned by
one another.   In an incomplete phase, when the
feelings are not yet synthesized and do not in
a sense know of one another, they are still so

formed as not only to allow but also to demand
unification with one another. Thus a sort of
pre-established harmony seems to reign over
them. The main point is that all the feelings
in an incomplete phase of an actual entity are
dominated by one common aim (viz. the realization of the particular subjective unity of feeling
constituting the actual entity in question), and
no incompatible feelings can be allowed within
a unitary process.

The second is the category of objective
identity. It says that there can be no duplication
of any element in the objective datum felt in the
final stage of satisfaction. In the completed
phase of the process, the actual entity is one
complex feeling, and in this unity of feeling one
element does not discharge diverse functions ; it
fills only one definite role. That is to say, one
element in the objective datum counts as one,
and not as two or many.

The third category, which is the counterpart
of the second category, is called the category of
objective diversity. It says that there can be no
coalescence of diverse elements in the objective
datum in the stage of satisfaction. If there are
two elements, they must have different functions ;
they cannot be two and yet perform one self-
identical function. The second category enjoins
against the duplication of the identical element
and the third against the identification of diverse
elements. If the second category says that one
cannot be many, the third category says that
many cannot be one.

The category of objective identity lays down
a condition which makes it necessary for the

diverse feelings of one and the same entity to be integrated in the final stage. In an incomplete phase one and the same entity, whether an actual entity or an eternal object, may be felt by different feelings. If in the final stage these different feelings remained unintegrated, the same element would appear in different roles and perform diverse functions. This it cannot do, according to the category of objective identity. So the different feelings with one common entity as the datum do not remain different in the completed phase, but are integrated into one feeling in which the one entity performs but one function. In other words, the many feelings of one entity in the incomplete phase turn into one feeling of the same in the completed phase.

We come next to the category of conceptual valuation, which is the fourth in the list. According to this category, from every physical feeling there arises a purely conceptual feeling of the eternal object which is exemplified in the actual entity or the nexus (of actual entities) physically felt. We know that an actual entity or a nexus of actual entities is something definite, and the form of its definiteness is an eternal object. Some eternal object is thus always exemplified in an actual entity or a nexus of actual entities. From a physical feeling of the actual entity or the nexus, there arises a conceptual feeling of the eternal object therein illustrated. This category says in substance that concepts are derived from sensations and that all sensitive experience leads to mental operations.

We may remind ourselves here that, in terms of this philosophy, the physical feelings give us

the physical pole, and the conceptual feelings the
mental pole, of the actual entity entertaining
these feelings.

The mental pole starts with conceptual reproduction. But this may lead to other conceptual
feelings which have for their data eternal objects
which are somewhat different from, although
related to, the eternal objects felt in the earlier
phase. This is what the fifth category, the
category of conceptual reversion, purports to say.
Subsequent to a physical feeling, we have a
conceptual feeling of the eternal object exemplified
in the datum of the physical feeling. Subsequent
to one or more such conceptual feelings, we may
have conceptual feelings of other eternal objects
which are partially identical with, and partially
different from, the eternal objects felt in the
earlier phase of the mental pole.

From our sensation of a thing we get (conceptually feel) the idea (eternal object) of what it is.
This is conceptual reproduction, as expressed by
the previous (fourth) category. But from our
idea of what the thing is, we may be led on to
think of other relevant possibilities which are not
actualized in the thing. From our idea of a shape
seen in a chair, we may be led to think of other
shapes, shapes which are different from, but
related to, the actual shape of the chair. We are
using in this example highly intellectual ideas to
explain what must be true even of a low-grade
mentality. The main point is that proximate
and relevant alternatives enter into a conceptual
feeling which derives itself from another conceptual feeling based on a physical feeling.

In many cases there may be only conceptual

reproduction without conceptual reversion, so that we are kept close to the original physical feeling. But in many cases we deviate from it also. We are not always content with the ideas delivered to us by the given fact, but may come to entertain new ideas on the suggestion of those derived from the fact. The new ideas are somewhat different from the ideas given by the fact, and in this sense there is reversion ; but they must also be similar in some sense.

We now come to the sixth category, the category of transmutation, which accounts for an important class of feelings, viz. transmuted feelings. In a transmuted feeling, we feel a nexus as one, and this feeling arises out of the many simple physical feelings of the actual entities composing the nexus. The nexus is felt as one, in contrast with an eternal object, or, in more familiar phraseology, as qualified by a universal. The transmutation of many physical feelings of many actual entities into one physical feeling of a nexus takes place in accordance with this category. It says that when one and the same conceptual feeling is derived impartially from many analogous simple physical feelings of various actual entities, then these feelings, both original and derived, physical and conceptual, get integrated or transmuted into one physical feeling of the nexus (constituted by the actual entities) in contrast with (i.e. qualified by) an eternal object which is the datum in the earlier conceptual feeling. First there arises a single conceptual feeling from many pure and hybrid physical feelings, and this may happen either by simple conceptual reproduction or by both

conceptual reproduction and conceptual reversion. Then as it arises impartially from the many
physical feelings, it leads to their integration into
one feeling in which the many data of the earlier
physical feelings are felt as one nexus. In the
original physical feelings, the actual entities are
surely felt in their diversity, but on account of
the similarity of their function, their difference
is overlooked in the transmuted feeling and they
are all felt under the aspect of a common eternal
object. By means of this transmutation, we are
relieved of all irrelevant details, and are enabled
to concentrate our attention on salient characters.
If nature never allowed such transmutation, we
should be simply bewildered and overwhelmed
by the infinite diversity and variety of things
pressing in upon us from all sides.

We see thus that by transmutation, many
actualities are felt as one and what is merely
possible or ideal comes to be felt as actual. The
many blades of grass of the original physical
feeling are felt as one grassy plot in the transmuted
feeling. The look of a flower suggests the idea
of softness to our mind, but by transmutation the
flower takes on a soft look, and softness, which is
merely ideal, comes to be seen (felt as actual) in
the flower.

The separation of mind and body has had
serious consequences for modern philosophy.
Whitehead believes that he has bridged the gulf
between mind and body by his doctrine of hybrid
physical feelings and transmuted feelings.

By these doctrines he makes physical feeling
give rise to conceptual feeling and conceptual
feeling pass into the category of physical feeling.

CHAPTER IX

FEELINGS (*continued*)

THE feelings we have so far considered do not involve consciousness. Consciousness appears in a higher kind of feelings, and we rise to those feelings through what is called propositional feeling. A propositional feeling as such does not involve consciousness, but if a feeling is to be conscious, a proposition must enter into its complex constitution. We shall now study the propositional and other higher feelings in this chapter.

A propositional feeling, as its name implies, is a feeling in which what we feel is a proposition. The feeling of a proposition is a propositional feeling. A proposition, as we know, is neither an actual entity nor an eternal object, but an eternal object understood in reference to certain actual entities. An eternal object by itself is understood in the absolutely general sense of " any ". It may appear anywhere in the actual world, and thus it refers in a very general sense to the actual world. A proposition, on the other hand, is understood only in reference to a group of actual entities which are its logical subjects. The eternal object, which appears in a proposition, still retains its accent of generality, but restricted within a limited area of actual entities.

An eternal object is neither true nor false, but a proposition is necessarily either true or false.

" Truth and falsehood always require some
element of sheer givenness ", and this element is
supplied by the actual entities, which are involved
in a proposition as its logical subjects.   It is thus
clear that propositions are complex entities
requiring in their composition both actual
entities and eternal objects.   This also implies
that new propositions come into being along with
new actual entities.   When determinate new
actual entities are brought into being by the
creative process, they appear with a determinate
group of possibilities which are definitely open
to them.   These possibilities (eternal objects)
restricted to them are propositions of which the
new actual entities are the logical subjects.

Since propositions are made up of actual entities
and eternal objects, it is evident that propositional
feelings involve the feelings of actual entities and
of eternal objects.   That is to say, there must be
already some physical and conceptual feelings in
order that a propositional feeling may arise.   One
cannot start all at once with a propositional
feeling.   It arises only in a late phase in the
process of the prehending subject.   In the earlier
stages there must be the requisite physical and
conceptual feelings, which are later integrated
into the propositional feeling.

The earlier stages of a propositional feeling are
analysed in this way.   First, there is a physical
feeling in which the actual entities are given
which are the logical subjects of the proposition.
This feeling is called the indicative feeling and it
provides the subject.   Second, there is another
physical feeling, involving an eternal object as
a determinant of the actual entity or entities felt

by it.   This feeling is called the physical recognition and it supplies the physical basis of the
conceptual feeling from which the predicate is
derived.   Third, there is a conceptual feeling of
the eternal object involved in the datum of the
second physical feeling.   This feeling is derived
from the second feeling according to the category
of conceptual valuation explained in the last
chapter.   This feeling provides the predicate.
Sometimes, however, the predicate is not exactly
what is exemplified in the datum of the second
physical feeling, but some other eternal object.
In that case, the conceptual feeling, derived
directly from the second feeling according to the
category of conceptual valuation, will not supply
the predicate.   For this we require another
conceptual feeling derived from this one according
to the category of conceptual reversion.   In
either case, the conceptual feeling which supplies
the predicate is called the predicative feeling.   If
the predicate is obtained from the third feeling,
then it is the same eternal object which defines
the object of the second physical feeling.   And
if the predicate is obtained from the reverted
conceptual feeling, which is the fourth feeling in
the above enumeration, then it is different from,
though related to, the eternal object involved in
the datum of the physical recognition (second
physical feeling).

The propositional feeling arises when the
indicative feeling is integrated with the predicative feeling ; and in this integration, the different
data of these different feelings are synthesized
into one datum, a proposition, for the integral
propositional feeling.   The synthesis is effected

through the elimination of certain aspects from the data of the earlier feelings. The actual entities given in the indicative feeling are reduced to a bare multiplicity in which each is a bare " it ", devoid of any definite character, because the eternal object which determined their definiteness and made them really into a nexus is eliminated. The object of the predicative feeling is deprived of its absolute generality, which pertains to every eternal object, and is restricted, or joined on, to the logical subjects. The indeterminateness of bare " its " is thus removed by their synthesis with the eternal object given by the predicative feeling.

In the above analysis of the earlier stages of the process leading to a propositional feeling, we have found two physical feelings and one or two conceptual feelings. The first of the physical feelings is the indicative feeling from which the logical subjects are derived, and the second is the physical recognition from which we derive the predicative feeling. If the predicative feeling is derived directly from the physical recognition by conceptual valuation, then we have only one conceptual feeling, and if it is derived by conceptual valuation and conceptual reversion, then we have two conceptual feelings.

If one and the same physical feeling enjoys the roles both of the indicative feeling and of the physical recognition, then the derived propositional feeling is called a perceptive feeling, because it predicates of its logical subjects a character which is derived from the way in which they are physically felt. If the two physical feelings are different, then the derived propositional feeling is called an imaginative feeling, because in this case there is no guarantee of any close relevance of the predicate to the logical subjects.   But there are degrees of difference, and the indicative feeling and the physical recognition may be widely divergent or almost identical, and so the distinction between perceptive feelings and imaginative feelings is not as sharp as might be supposed.

The proposition given in a perceptive feeling is not necessarily true, because the predicate may be obtained by reversion, in which case it is not what actually determines the definiteness of the logical subjects.   But if there is no reversion at any stage, then the proposition perceptively felt is true.

A proposition is no doubt either true or false, but to be true or false is not the primary function of a proposition.   Its primary function is to be interesting or, as Whitehead expresses it, to be a lure for feeling.   Consequently, the subjective form of a propositional feeling involves what is called " decision ", that is, " adversion " or " aversion ".   There is a tendency towards the realization of the possibility involved in the proposition or a tendency in the opposite direction.

A propositional feeling is not necessarily characterized by consciousness.   Consciousness properly appears only in the case of intellectual feelings which are a variety of comparative feelings.   These feelings remain to be considered now.

All the higher feelings which are very complex in character come under comparative feelings.

The datum in them all is some contrast between what is and what may be, between actuality and a proposition or an eternal object. This determines how they come into being. Actualities are given in physical feelings, and propositions and eternal objects are given in propositional and conceptual feelings respectively. So a comparative feeling arises by the integration of a physical feeling with a propositional or a conceptual feeling. Thus there are two simple types of comparative feelings. In one type we have the integration of a propositional feeling with the physical (indicative) feeling from which it is partly derived. The feelings of this type are called intellectual feelings. In the other type we have the integration of a conceptual feeling with the basic physical feeling from which it is derived either by simple conceptual valuation or by both conceptual valuation and conceptual reversion. The feelings of this type are called " physical purposes ".

Let us consider the intellectual feelings first, as they follow, in natural sequence, the propositional feelings which we considered above. We must remember here that there are two kinds of propositional feelings, one perceptive and the other imaginative. The integration of a perceptive feeling with the indicative feeling gives rise to what is called " conscious perception " and the integration of an imaginative feeling with the indicative feeling gives rise to what is called intuitive judgment. These are the two varieties of intellectual feelings.

In all comparative feelings, the datum, or what is felt, is a contrast. This is why, I suppose, they are called comparative feelings. In an intellectual feeling the contrast felt is between a nexus of actual entities and a proposition which has for its logical subjects the members of the nexus. A contrast is a kind of unity with distinct factors within it. The factors here involved are the nexus and the proposition, and the unity of the contrast arises from the fact that the same entities are felt as functioning in different ways. The actual entities of the nexus, for instance, are felt in the physical feeling as actual facts, and the same appear in the propositional feeling as logical subjects, as mere food for a possibility. Both the physical feeling and the propositional feeling have a common subject, and this is why they can be integrated. In the integrated feeling, the same entities cannot appear in different roles, according to the category of objective identity (see page 109). In one and the same feeling the same entities cannot separately appear as actual and as possible. Therefore the actual entities, given in one way in the physical feeling and in a different way in the propositional feeling, are not given different roles in the integrated feeling, but are endowed with one role of a two-way functioning, or one role with a two-way aspect. " This two-way aspect is unified as contrast."[1] This contrast is also called the affirmation-negation contrast. " It is the contrast between the affirmation of objectified fact in the physical feeling, and the mere potentiality, which is the negation of such affirmation, in the propositional feeling."[2]

[1] *Process and Reality*, p. 377.
[2] Ibid., p. 377.

Consciousness is the subjective form of the feeling which feels this contrast. Although consciousness properly belongs to intellectual feelings, and arises by reason of such feelings, it is shared in common by the unity of all feelings in the final stage of satisfaction ; all feelings acquire their quota of irradiation in consciousness.

Our experience does not begin with consciousness, but only rises up to it on occasions. And when consciousness is attained, one does not remain long at the white-hot stage of clear consciousness ; and even when consciousness is at its brightest there is only a small core, which is clearly illuminated, with a wide margin of intense experience in dim apprehension. Whitehead's theory seeks to square up with these facts of experience.

In the case of a conscious perception, we have a basic physical feeling from which a propositional feeling of the perceptive kind arises, and then gets integrated with the original physical feeling. We know that in the case of a perceptive propositional feeling, one and the same physical feeling serves both as the indicative feeling and as the physical recognition. In other words, when the logical subjects and the predicate are derived from the same physical feeling, the resulting propositional feeling is perceptive. It is direct and authentic when the predicate of the proposition, felt by it, is actually exemplified in the nexus of actual entities physically felt, and is directly derived from the physical feeling without any reversion. In some cases, although the same physical feeling supplies the logical subjects and the predicate, the predicate is derived by way of reversion and is not exactly what is exemplified in the nexus of actual entities given in the physical feeling. The resulting feeling is perceptive but erroneous, perceptive because it is based on one and the same physical feeling, and erroneous because the predicate of the proposition felt by it is not exemplified in the actual entities given in the physical feeling.

In any case when the proposition, given in the perceptive propositional feeling, is contrasted with the actual entities given in the original physical feeling, we get conscious perception which feels the contrast. A proposition is a possibility limited to a group of actual entities. Conscious perception thus feels the contrast of a nexus as fact with a possibility derived from the nexus and limited to it and exemplified in it. In wrong perception, this exemplification fails, because the predicate or the requisite eternal object is derived by way of reversion from the original physical feeling. Perception thus is not necessarily right, and requires to be examined before its evidence can be accepted. We have to see, when we rely on a perception, that it is based on a direct authentic perceptive feeling and has not involved reversion at any stage.

Intuitive judgment arises from the integration of an imaginative feeling with the indicative feeling. Just as an imaginative feeling is not very sharply distinguished from a perceptive feeling, so is intuitive judgment not wholly different from conscious perception. In intuitive judgment as well as in conscious perception we have the integration of a physical feeling and a propositional feeling which are such that the actual entities, felt in the physical feeling, are the logical subjects of the proposition which is felt in the propositional feeling.   In the case of conscious perception, the propositional feeling is derived from one and the same physical feeling, whereas in the case of intuitive judgment, the propositional feeling is based on two physical feelings, one of which is the indicative feeling and the other the physical recognition.   The difference between conscious perception and intuitive judgment is based ultimately on the difference between the two physical feelings which serve as the indicative feeling and the physical recognition. If one and the same feeling serves the purposes of both, we have conscious perception ; and if the indicative feeling and the physical recognition are two distinct feelings, they give rise to intuitive judgment.   But the difference between the two physical feelings may be very slight, the eternal object involved in the physical recognition may be almost identical with what is exemplified in the nexus of actual entities given in the indicative feeling.   In that case, there will be very little difference between the resulting intuitive judgment and the corresponding conscious perception.

Intellectual feelings involving judgment are of three different forms, (i) yes-form, (ii) no-form, and (iii) suspense-form.

In all such feelings, what is felt is the contrast between an objectified nexus and a proposition whose logical subjects make up the nexus.   In the feelings of the yes-form the contrast felt involves also the identity of the pattern of the nexus with the predicate of the proposition.   In the feelings of the no-form, the contrast involves incompatible diversity between the pattern (what is exemplified in the nexus) and the predicate. In the feelings of the suspense-form, the contrast involves neither identity nor incompatibility between the pattern and the predicate. This shows that there are not merely affirmative and negative judgments, but there are suspended judgments also. Such judgments are essential to scientific progress.

Consciousness is illustrated in all these feelings, as they all involve affirmation-negation contrast. " The triumph of consciousness ", however, as Whitehead observes, " comes with the negative intuitive judgment."[1] The affirmation-negation contrast is present in conscious perception also. But there the contrast is between a fact and a possibility which is also illustrated in the fact, and so the negative element is not so explicit there. It is very explicit in negative judgment.

We may now consider the other kind of comparative feelings which are called physical purposes. They are more primitive than intellectual feelings, and do not involve consciousness unless they are combined with other feelings which are conscious.

Physical purposes arise through the integration of conceptual feelings with physical feelings. The contrast which is felt in a physical purpose is between a nexus physically felt and an eternal object conceptually valued. The eternal object is derived from the physical feeling either by mere conceptual valuation or by conceptual valuation and conceptual reversion. When there is a physical feeling of certain actual entities,

[1] *Process and Reality*, p. 387.

there arises a conceptual feeling of the eternal object exemplified in those actual entities. Sometimes by reversion, what is felt in the subsequent conceptual feeling is not exactly the eternal object which is illustrated in the nexus physically felt, but some other eternal object which is somewhat different from the one illustrated in the nexus, but relevant to the situation. This determines the two species of physical purposes, one involving no reversion, and the other involving reversion, in the mental pole.

In the case of a physical purpose of the first species, we have, first, a physical feeling and, second, a conceptual feeling arising from the physical feeling according to the category of conceptual valuation, and then the two feelings are integrated to form a physical purpose. What is felt in a physical purpose is, as we have said, a contrast between a nexus and an eternal object. In this case the eternal object conceptually valued is also exemplified as the pattern of the nexus given in the physical feeling. A conceptual feeling is a valuation, involving adversion or aversion. Re-enaction or repetition is the subjective form of a physical feeling. Now when a conceptual feeling, involving adversion, is combined with the physical feeling from which it is derived, the creative process gains some additional force to re-enact or reproduce what is physically felt, beyond the present feeling in the future. Enduring objects are generated in this way. When the conceptual feeling involves aversion, the reproductive force of the creative process is enfeebled, and there is a tendency to eliminate the content.

There is some complexity in the second species of physical purposes. We have already explained six categoreal conditions. The remaining two categories may be briefly explained here, which find their application in these physical purposes. These categories are the category of subjective harmony and the category of subjective intensity. The category of subjective harmony says that the subjective forms of different conceptual feelings are " mutually determined by their adaptation to be joint elements in a satisfaction aimed at by the subject ".[1] This means that there cannot be incompatible valuations of conceptual feelings which enter into one satisfaction. They should be adapted to one another and this is dictated by the subjective aim which they together satisfy in one satisfaction. The category of subjective intensity says that the subjective aim, operating in the origination of conceptual feelings, is " intensity of feeling in the immediate subject and in the relevant future ".[2] Now conceptual feelings arise only with a view to realizing some intensity of feeling. And intensity of feeling results from balanced complexity or contrasts.

Now, in the case of the second species of physical purposes, which may be called complex physical purposes, in distinction from the simple ones considered before, we have first a physical feeling, and, second, a primary conceptual feeling derived by simple conceptual valuation from the first feeling, and, third, a reverted conceptual feeling whose datum is somewhat different from the datum of the primary conceptual feeling, and

[1] *Process and Reality*, p. 360.
[2] Ibid., p. 393.

so is not exactly what is exemplified as the pattern of the nexus felt in the original physical feeling. The integration of the physical feeling, the primary conceptual feeling and the secondary (or reverted) conceptual feeling produces a complex physical purpose.

The subjective forms of the two conceptual feelings should be adapted to each other (in accordance with the category of subjective harmony) so as to fulfil the subjective aim. The combination of the physical feeling with the primary conceptual feeling alone would give rise merely to a simple physical purpose, but the appearance of a reverted conceptual feeling introduces a complex physical purpose. And this reverted feeling appears in order that it may contribute to some intensity of feeling by providing a new contrast. This is in accordance with the category of subjective intensity. The reverted conceptual feeling introduces a new eternal object which is in contrast with the eternal object given in the primary conceptual feeling. The introduction of conceptual contrast (of two eternal objects) heightens the scale of subjective intensity, and the heightened subjective intensity is concentrated upon the reverted feeling, as it is the novel factor which introduces the contrast. When the life of an enduring object is dominated by complex physical purpose, this emphasis on the reverted conceptual feeling enables it to be transmitted into the next occasion as a physical feeling according to the category of transmutation. And this transmuted physical feeling leads to a reverted conceptual feeling, which has for its datum the pattern of the original physical feeling.

As the transmuted physical feeling is but the previous reverted conceptual feeling, its pattern is in contrast with the pattern of the original physical feeling.   So there are successive physical feelings of contrasted patterns.   " Thus   . . . there is a chain of contrast in the physical feelings of the successive occasions ", and " in each occasion there is the physical feeling with its primary valuation in contrast with the reverted conceptual feeling ".[1]

Rhythm and vibration, so important in the physical world, are to be explained by this theory of complex physical purpose.

<hr>

[1] *Process and Reality*, p. 395.

CHAPTER X

PERCEPTION

SOMETHING has been said about perception already, in a bald and technical manner, in the previous chapter. The importance attached to the topic in contemporary philosophy demands that we should know in greater detail and more explicitly what Whitehead has to say on the subject.

There is an apparent simplicity about the fact of perception. We open our eyes and see things around us, and there appears nothing mysterious about the matter. But do we really see the things ? Certain portions of the contemporary world appear, no doubt, illustrated by certain sensa, but that there are things identified with these sensa does not appear at all to be immediately given. But there is not the least doubt that whenever we apprehend certain sensa, we pass on to the things which stand behind, or are identified with, the sensa. When, for instance, we see a particular coloured shape, we at once say it is a chair.

It may be supposed that we get to the notion of chair from the perception of the colour and the shape, by means of inference. But the facts do not support this theory. It is only by a difficult train of reasoning that we can be led, if at all, from the apprehension of the coloured shape to the notion of the chair. Such highly

intellectual operation is not possible in the case
of lower animals. But even a dog on the
apprehension of the coloured shape would at
once take it to be a chair and behave towards it
accordingly. This shows clearly that to get to
the chair from the coloured shape, one does not
need to perform any such highly intellectual act
as inference.

Moreover, although we ordinary people pass
immediately to the idea of the chair from the
apprehension of the coloured shape, an artist,
who is trained in his profession, may stop at the
contemplation of the beautiful colour and shape,
and may not at once pass on to the idea of
the chair.

On the theory of inference, we have to suppose
that the artist has been restrained from performing
the inference by his elaborate artistic training.
But one does not need to be trained merely to
refrain from some difficult mental work. One
naturally avoids such work even without any
training. Thus it is clear that our transition
from the apprehension of the coloured shape to
the idea of the chair is not mediated or accom-
panied by any intellectual operation. Constituted as we are, we naturally pass on from the one
to the other.

But to pass from the one to the other involves
a process. We may legitimately ask what
exactly is the process by which we get from the
one to the other. And, further, if by sense-
perception we get the coloured shape only, how
is it then possible to get to the notion of the chair
which is not presented at all ? We cannot pass
from the given to the not-given except through

inference, and inference is not allowed here. How does Whitehead answer these questions ?

What is commonly called perception is described by him as symbolic reference. The coloured shape is used as the symbol for the chair, and when the coloured shape is given by sense-perception, we pass by symbolic reference from the coloured shape to the chair. But we can pass from the one to the other when the other is also given. If the other remains ungiven, how can we ever pass on to it ? Whitehead here says that the chair is also given, as the coloured shape is given, but the two are not given in the same way. We get to them in two different modes of perception. In this connection Whitehead develops his theory of the two pure modes of perception called the mode of presentational immediacy and the mode of causal efficacy, whose synthesis in a mixed mode constitutes symbolic reference or our ordinary perception.

" Presentational immediacy is our perception of the contemporary world by means of the senses."[1] It does not involve any element of interpretation, and is not therefore liable to error. Our ordinary perceptual experience is always mixed up with a good deal of interpretation. We take certain things to mean certain other things. So it is very difficult to get down to the level of pure presentational immediacy. But if we could keep out all mental interference, and could attend merely to what the senses themselves declared, we should be in the mode of presentational immediacy. The point is that by presentational immediacy we are made aware of the

[1] *Process and Reality*, p. 441.

contemporary world as illustrated, or made vivid, by certain sensa. While we are in this mode, we do not know what the sensa stand for, and we see them merely disposed in a particular manner.

Philosophers have generally taken presentational immediacy to be the primary fact in perception, and have held that whatever is to be posited in the perceived world should be derivable from this fact. In opposition to this view, Whitehead holds that presentational immediacy is not the only mode by which we know the objective world, but there is another primary mode, more fundamental than presentational immediacy, which is at the root of all our objective experience. Our ordinary perception arises out of an interplay between these two pure modes. He calls the latter mode the mode of causal efficacy. It may also be called causal feeling.

Credit must be given to Whitehead for drawing our pointed attention to this fundamental and important aspect of experience. Both Kant and Hume ignored the presence of any primary causal feeling in our experience. They did not think that causality could be felt. With Kant it was a form of thought, and with Hume it was a habit of thought.

It is true that if we confine ourselves to the evidence of presentational immediacy, we never come across any percept which bears the mark of causality in it ; and these philosophers did not recognize any other mode. But our experience seems to show that we have clearly some feeling of causality. When in a dark room, the electric light is suddenly turned on, and a man is made to blink, his whole experience does not consist merely in seeing the flash and in the experience of blinking ; but he feels the flash making him blink. If he were afterwards to be asked as to how he knew that the flash made him blink, he would surely reply that he knew because he felt it so. It is thus difficult to deny some direct feeling of causality.

Moreover, when we see a thing we not only feel the visual sensum, but we also feel that we are seeing it with the eye. When we taste, we feel we are tasting with the palate ; when we smell we feel we are smelling with the nose. The feeling of " with " in respect of any sense-organ is the feeling of the causal efficacy of the sense-organ in the matter of the relevant sensum given by presentational immediacy.

The feeling of causal efficacy appears to be present in some dim form in very low forms of animal life and even in vegetables, which give no evidence of perception in the mode of presentational immediacy. " A jellyfish advances and withdraws, and in so doing exhibits some perception of causal relationship with the world beyond itself ; a plant grows downwards to the damp earth, and upwards towards the light."[1] We have no reason to suppose that these lowly creatures ever have any definite percepts in the mode of presentational immediacy, but from the way they behave towards their surroundings, we cannot but attribute to them some dim feeling of causal relationship.

Philosophers have found it easy to ignore the feeling of causal efficacy, because they have not

[1] *Process and Reality*, p. 249.

properly considered the real character of time. We know time primarily as the succession of our acts of experience, and derivatively as the succession of events objectively perceived in those acts. But there is no such thing as mere succession. Succession in the concrete is the conformation of one event to another, of the later to the earlier. There is no lapse of empty time, but only succession of events, which again means that every event is derived from its predecessor to which it conforms. The flow of time is really this causal flow of events, in which the later events have to conform to the earlier ones. The irreversibility of time means really the irreversibility of this causal relationship. The idea of empty time, mere succession, is an abstraction from this concrete fact.

That the present is inevitably the effect of the past can be seen clearly if we consider our present state in relation to what has just gone before it. When we begin pronouncing a word, we feel compelled to finish it. In the creative advance, we are rushed on from state to state, and our present being is clearly the outcome of our immediate past. And we have a deep and direct feeling of the derivation of our present state from the state which precedes it. This sense of causal derivation is apt to be missed when we spread our survey over a longer interval of time. We may not see how to-day is made by yesterday. But when we confine our attention to successive states separated by the shortest possible time, we clearly see that the later state is the result of the earlier one. This we see not by any mystical insight, but by a simple direct feeling, the feeling of the

derivation of our present being from our
immediate past self.

This causal feeling is closely entwined with all
our primitive emotions. Anger, hatred, fear,
love and hunger all involve the primitive
functioning of " retreat from " or " expansion
towards ". They are in fact only different
forms of either of these functions. But " retreat
from " or " expansion towards " always implies
some entity, other than ourselves, from which we
can retreat or towards which we can expand.
We cannot retreat merely from ourselves. Thus
in experiencing these emotions, we clearly realize
the reactions of other actual things on ourselves.
We feel them in their causal efficacy in relation
to our experience. When I hate, I hate a man
or some other being that can causally affect me
and is felt as doing so, and not a collection of
sense-data that are given in presentational
immediacy. It is thus clear that the feeling of
causal efficacy is an element in the ultimate
texture of our experience. This feeling, although
always deep and inescapable, and heavy with
emotion, fails to win its due measure of recognition from us, because our attention is captured by
the clarity and definiteness, the superficial
brightness in the literal sense, of what we get in
the mode of presentational immediacy.

Each of these modes has its distinctive character. The percepta in the mode of causal
efficacy are vague and indistinct, not to be
controlled and heavy with emotion ; but the
percepta in the mode of presentational immediacy
are distinct and definite, and also controllable.
The former mode produces a sense of derivation

from the immediate past, and of passage to the immediate future, and thus gives us a distinct feeling of past and future. In the latter mode, there is no reference to past or future. Merely from a datum in presentational immediacy we have no means of knowing on which side of it lies past and on which side future. In fact, whether there are such sides or directions, we cannot know in this mode. We are subject to the percepta in the mode of causal efficacy, but we can adjust our percepta in the other mode. The respective roles of these modes, as Whitehead points out, are aptly exemplified by the fact that all scientific observations are made in the mode of presentational immediacy, whereas all scientific theory is expressed in terms of entities that can be perceived only in the mode of causal efficacy. This brings out clearly that what we know about " chiefly resides in those aspects of the world disclosed in causal efficacy ", and what we can distinctly register is provided by the percepta in the other mode.

Let us now try to understand how symbolic reference arises out of an interplay between these two modes. In all symbolism we have two things, the symbol and the meaning. These are relative terms understood in reference to each other. In themselves, they are components of some experience, usually percepta, and are related by way of symbol and meaning in virtue of some specific function. A perceptum is a symbol when it evokes consciousness, belief and behaviour proper to another perceptum, which is its meaning. The two percepta may be given in the same mode, and either of them may be used as the symbol or the meaning. But in symbolic reference we have two different species of percepta given in different modes, and what is given by presentational immediacy is used as the symbol for what is given by causal efficacy and not vice versa.

When two percepta are related as symbol and meaning, they may be spoken of as correlates. Now, " there is ' symbolic reference ' between the two species when the perception of a member of one species evokes its correlate in the other species, and precipitates upon this correlate the fusion of feelings, emotions, and derivative actions, which belong to either of the pair of correlates ".[1] That from which symbolic reference starts is called the symbol and that with which it ends is called the meaning.

When I see a friend coming to me and become therefore glad, what really happens is that I perceive in the mode of presentational immediacy some shape and colour, and this evokes in me the consciousness of my friend, belief in his near presence and the consequent gladness. The coloured shape itself, presented to sight, is not the friend who is an actual being and can be felt only by a causal feeling. The coloured shape is used as the symbol of the actual person, and the perception of it blends itself with that of the actual being given in causal efficacy. In fact, in ordinary perception, we make no distinction between the coloured shape and the actual person. This is how symbolic reference works. We project the sensum on to the physical nexus causally felt, and take it (the sensum) as the

[1] *Process and Reality*, p. 255.

representative, in clear consciousness, of what is
vaguely, but deeply, felt in causal efficacy.

Symbolic reference presupposes some definite
connection between the symbol and the meaning.
We cannot symbolically refer anything to anything, but such reference is possible only between
those things which have some common elements.
Let us see what common elements there are
between the data of causal efficacy and those of
presentational immediacy.

One common ground is the presented locus.
When, for instance, a grey stone is perceived,
it is perceived in some spatial position. The
locus of it is felt in both causal efficacy and
presentational immediacy. The contemporary
locus, which is presented in immediacy, cannot, of
course, be felt directly in causal efficacy, because
we can causally feel only what is past, and causal
independence is the very meaning of contemporaneity. The prehending subject feels its own
past directly in causal feeling, but its own past
is largely identical with the past of the contemporary locus. So in feeling its own past, the
prehending subject feels the past of the contemporary locus also ; and the contemporary locus
is only a continuation of its past, and thus in
feeling the causal past of the contemporary locus,
we may be said to feel indirectly the contemporary
locus itself. The locus, from the standpoint of
its past or of the prehending subject, is a real
potentiality (see page 76), and it is perceived
vaguely in causal efficacy as exemplifying those
spatial relations involved in the real potentiality.
In presentational immediacy, the locus is perceived
directly and distinctly under the illustration of

the sensa.   Thus the locus perceived differently
in the two modes is one common ground for the
symbolic reference.

The datum of presentational immediacy is
quite definite as regards its geometrical or
spatial relation.   We perceive distinctly in what
geometrical relation, at least with the body, it
lies.   But the datum of a causal feeling lacks this
distinctness.   Without the assistance given by
presentational immediacy we do not know where
the datum of a causal feeling is situated.   Its
geometrical relations never come out clearly in
causal efficacy.   In the case of the different parts
of the body, however, it is different.   Here the
indistinctness, to some extent at least, is removed.
When we see with our eyes, the region of the
causal efficacy (i.e. the eye) is no longer indefinite.
The eye-strain, given in presentational immediacy
has, by itself, no better claim to be associated with
sight than any stomach-ache which we may be
feeling at the time.   But the eye-strain is
connected with sight, because the region defined
by the feeling of the strain (in presentational
immediacy) is identical with the region which is
felt in its causal efficacy in the matter of sight.
Thus the causal feeling, in respect of the different
parts of the body, unlike an ordinary causal
feeling, is able to define the geometrical relations
of its data.   The animal body is the central
ground underlying all symbolic reference.   In it
the parts are defined by causal efficacy as well as
by presentational immediacy, and the common
ground between them, the identity of the region,
necessary for symbolic reference, is easily found.

Another ground of correlation is the presence

of the same eternal object in the two modes of
perception. The sensum, for instance, given
by the efficacity of the eye, is the same as what
we perceive as illustrating the locus presented in
immediacy. When we perceive a stone as grey,
the eternal object grey defines the locus, presented
in immediacy, as well as the sensum given by the
efficacity of the eye. This identity of the
eternal object correlates the datum in one mode
of perception with the datum of the other mode,
and on the basis of this correlation both are
blended together in symbolic reference.

We have said that the presented locus is
illustrated by sensa, and we also say that a
sensum is derived from the efficacity of a sense-
organ, e.g. the eye. What, then, really is a
sensum ? A sensum is not primarily what we
perceive outside. It is primarily a mode of
feeling. The red we seem to see in an object
is really a quality of the feeling by which the
object is apprehended. Instead of saying that
we feel the red in the object, we should rather say
that we have a red feeling of the object. Whitehead thinks that the notion of sensa as forms of
feelings or " qualifications of affective tones " is
fairly obvious to common sense. " A red-
irritation is prevalent among nerve-racked people
and among bulls."[1] Our primary experience of
a sensum is that of a type of subjective feeling,
but " our developed consciousness fastens on the
sensum as datum ". We begin by having a
smelly feeling and it is developed by mentality
into the feeling of a smell. The sensa are thus
qualitative characters of effective tones inherent

[1] *Adventures of Ideas*, p. 315.

in bodily functionings, and are transmuted into characters of presented regions. The regions are perceived as associated with characters that are also shared by the subjective forms of feeling.

In the mode of presentational immediacy, the sensa are given for the percipient, but they are not given by the contemporary region which is seen as illustrated by them. There can be no transaction of " give and take " between contemporary events, because they are causally independent. So if a sensum is to be given for an actual entity, it must be derived from its past actual occasions. The ultimate percipient occasion is somewhere in the brain, and whatever is given for it, is inherited by it, through a line of succession from its predecessors. There is " a historic route of inheritance, from actual occasion to succeeding actual occasion, first physically in the external environment, then physiologically— through the eye in the case of visual data—up the nerves, into the brain ".[1] A shade of colour is thus first a mode of feeling in the eye. This sensum as a form of feeling is transmitted from occasion to occasion. And a feeling never loses its reference to the point of its origin. It has always what is called a vector character. The colour-sensum is a mode of feeling in the eye, but the feeling also says that it has come from an external object. Again, just as the sensa are given, the geometrical relations are also given. This makes it possible to refer a sensum to a definite locus.

When we perceive a grey stone, the grey sensum, as a mode of feeling in the eye, is not

[1] *Process and Reality*, p. 241.

generated by the contemporary stony occasion. We may recall here that what we call a stone is properly a historic route of stony occasions, and that whatever is derived or inherited from it must be due to the past actual occasions in the route and not to its contemporary member. The line of inheritance starts from some past actual occasion in the region of the stone, and ends with the concrescence of an actual occasion in the brain which is the percipient subject. The line takes a critical turn at the retina, from where a new kind of occasions begin to propagate themselves. The percipient occasion inherits and absorbs in the first instance all that has come from this long line of succession. In a supplemental stage, in virtue of the originative power of the concrescent percipient, the locus of the stone and the feeling in the eye (the grey sensum) are given particular prominence, because the line of inheritance started from that locus, and it took a critical turn at the eye, and the locus and the sensum appear as blended together.

The contemporary region is not actually a datum in any feeling. It is a " real potentiality " for the earlier occasions which are actually felt. The extensive relations, which define the actual occasions constituting the contemporary region, are what were " really possible " for their predecessors which are actually felt. By transmutation this possibility appears as an actuality, and the ungiven contemporary appears as given. The term stone, which stands for the historic route of stony occasions, is applied also to the presented locus, because it is assumed that the historic route is continued up to the contemporary region.

We have said that in presentational immediacy the contemporary region appears under the illustration of a sensum. Whether there is anything actual behind this appearance or whether it is a mere empty appearance is not disclosed in this mode. It is by symbolic reference that the sensum is joined to the actual entity, which is causally felt, or to its contemporary representative. We have to do here with the locus and the sensum. The locus is determined by its geometrical relationships. These relationships are also felt in the body. Whitehead calls such feelings " strains ". So what we are concerned with in a perception of this kind is a certain state of geometrical strain in the body together with a certain qualitative physiological excitement in the cells of the body. " The geometrical details of the projected sense-perception depend on the geometrical strains in the body, the qualitative sensa depend on the physiological excitements of the requisite cells in the body."[1]

We thus see that " the perceptions are functions of the bodily states ". What we primarily apprehend are the parts of the body entertaining feelings of different kinds (that is, as differently affected). These feelings in different parts of the body bear evidence of their origin, i.e. have a vector character. And these are later on elaborated, through presentational immediacy and symbolic reference, into perceptions of external objects.

There is no mistake in any of the two pure modes. What is causally felt or inherited from

[1] *Process and Reality*, p. 178.

the settled past is clearly what is so inherited.
The datum here by definition is a fact.   What
is perceived in presentational immediacy also
admits of no doubt.   In this mode, we have
merely the presentation of a locus illustrated by
a sensum.   If I see a grey region in front of me,
there can be nothing wrong merely in my
enjoying the sensum in that region, whether or
not there be anything like a stone in that place.
Nothing is presupposed in this mode as to the
presence or absence of any actual entity at the
place which is seen under the illustration of the
sensum.   We lay ourselves open to error only
when we are led by symbolic reference and make
what we perceive in presentational immediacy
interpretative of what we feel in causal efficacy.

And yet symbolic reference is not an act of
conscious interpretation.   " The two modes are
unified by a blind symbolic reference by which
supplemental feelings derived from the intensive,
but vague, mode of efficacity are precipitated
upon the distinct regions illustrated in the mode
of immediacy."[1]   By this integration of two
modes, what is intensely but vaguely felt (in
the mode of efficacity) is made distinct and clear,
and what is felt clearly but without depth (in the
mode of immediacy) is made deep and intense.

The symbolic reference is so natural and
instinctive that it is always difficult to discern
what is really given in the pure mode of immediacy.   The supplemental feelings, derived from
the primary data of the causal feeling, are not
due to any conscious process, but only to bodily
functions.   The symbolic reference or perception

[1] *Process and Reality*, p. 254.

in the mixed mode is right when the feelings produced by the bodily functions are relevant to the real state of external things. There is error when the feelings have but slight reference to the real state of things. Perceptual error thus is not due to any intellectual defect, but only to a faulty bodily mechanism. The rightness or wrongness of a perception cannot be discerned in the act of perception itself. It can be determined only by pragmatic tests.

Chapter XI

TRUTH

WE ended the last chapter by saying that the rightness or wrongness of a perception is to be determined by pragmatic tests. From the point of view of knowledge, the rightness or wrongness of a perception is its truth or falsehood. And the question at once suggests itself whether the meaning of truth itself is pragmatic. Whitehead goes so far as to admit that " it is hardly an exaggeration to say that the very meaning of truth is pragmatic ".[1] But he rightly points out that " though the statement is hardly an exaggeration, still it is an exaggeration ". We must then enquire what exactly is the meaning of truth in Whitehead's philosophy.

The idea of truth becomes significant when a distinction has emerged between reality and appearance. " Reality is just itself, and it is nonsense to ask whether it be true or false."[2] We can, however, ask about an appearance whether it is true or false. But what is reality ? And what is appearance ?

The settled past, the stubborn fact, the given actual world from which any actual occasion takes its rise, is the reality for that occasion. We know that the concrescence of an actual occasion begins by entertaining as objective contents the

[1] *Process and Reality*, p. 255.
[2] *Adventure of Ideas*, p. 309.

already constituted actualities falling within its
actual world. For every actual occasion there
is some given settled fact from which it arises
and to which it has to conform. For it, this is
the reality.

But an actual occasion is not wholly under the
domination of its predecessors ; it is not merely
a creature of the past. It has its own originative
freedom, in virtue of which it effects new syntheses
of the contents received from the antecedent
world. By its conceptual activities it invests
the given world with a novel aspect. Thus, for
instance, by integrating a physical feeling with
a conceptual feeling, a nexus of actual entities,
at first physically felt, is made to appear in the
light of a proposition. The nexus undergoes a
transformation of character when it becomes
a factor in a proposition. In symbolic reference
or what we call sense-perception, a region appears
under the aspect of some sensa which are derived
primarily from the subjective feelings of the
percipient subject. At least the region appears
with qualities that were not given in the primary
physical feelings of the actual entities which
constitute the region.

We see thus that tnere is a difference between
the objective contents received in the initial stage
by an actual occasion from its antecedent world,
and the objective contents which result from the
various acts of co-ordination and supplementation performed by the actual occasion upon the
initial data. The contents received in the
physical pole do not remain entirely unchanged
when they have been worked upon by the mental
pole. We have seen that at least in the case of

higher grades of actual occasions, the objective
contents, initially received in the physical pole,
are greatly transformed by the contributions
received from the mental pole.   By appearance
we understand the latter aspect of the objective
contents when they have been worked upon by
the mental pole.   In the first phase, an actual
occasion is confronted with reality, but at the
end the reality is transformed into appearance
through the ideal activities of its mental pole.
Thus if reality means merely the actual, in
appearance we have a fusion of the ideal with
the actual.

From the fact that appearance is due to the
activities of the mental pole, we can easily see
that there can be no effective appearance for
organisms that are possessed of a very low grade
of mentality.   Thus in the inorganic world,
where the physical feelings are all-important,
that is, where physical influences are merely
received and transmitted, with practically no
addition from the operation of the mental pole,
we have no reason to suppose that there are any
effective appearances.

In our case, however, especially in our conscious perceptions, appearance is of dominating
importance, so much so that many people have
supposed that we have acquaintance with reality
only through appearance.   We have seen that
this is not the case.   We know reality more
deeply in our causal feelings than through
appearance.   But it cannot be denied that if
clearness and distinctness is the ideal of knowledge
it is fulfilled only in the case of appearance.

Two points of distinction between appearance

and reality may be mentioned here. First,
reality as felt is in the past, whereas appearance
is in the present. The second point of distinction
is that appearance is simpler than reality. There
is an element of transmutation in every appearance. What is complex in reality becomes
simple in appearance. A region appears as one
and undivided, while in reality it is made up of
many actualities which are distinct from one
another. Whitehead therefore says that " appearance is an incredibly simplified edition of
reality ".[1]

The qualification of truth or falsehood is
properly applicable to appearance, according as
it conforms or does not conform to reality. We
have to note here that the truth-relation is not
between subjective knowledge and objective
content, but between two objective contents,
when one of them conforms to the other. Reality
is an objective content, so is appearance, and they
are combined in a truth-relation when appearance
conforms to reality.

But what is the meaning of conformation here ?
One thing may be said to conform to another
when there is a common element present in them
both. Without referring to appearance in particular, Whitehead defines the truth-relation
generally in the following way. When two
objects are such that neither is a component of
the other and their composite natures include
a common factor, then they can be said to have
a truth-relation to each other. Or, as he says,
" A truth-relation will be said to connect the
objective contents of two prehensions when one

[1] *Adventures of Ideas*, p. 273.

and the same identical pattern can be abstracted from both of them."[1] We know that reality is prehended in the first phase and appearance in a later phase, and they are in a truth-relation when both reality and appearance severally participate in the same pattern. When this is the case, it is evident that our knowledge about one of the facts in a truth-relation involves knowledge about the other fact also, so far as the truth-relation extends.

We do not know truth by itself ; we know only of a truth-relation. When we say that an appearance is true, all that we mean is that the appearance sustains a truth-relation, as defined above, with the reality which underlies it or from which it has been derived.

Propositions and sense-perception provide two conspicuous examples of truth-relation, understood in the above sense. We have said that truth is to be understood in connection with appearance. And in the case of propositions we have not, it is true, the sort of appearance that is available in the case of sense-perception. Still, we have to recognize that a proposition is an extreme case of appearance. The actual entities, which are the logical subjects of a proposition, are conceived in the guise of illustrating the predicate. As factors in a proposition, they are not felt in their real actual character but only as a field for the realization of a possibility. They are felt, as it were, with the shade of possibility colouring their being.

A proposition is true when it has the truth-relation with the nexus which provides its logical

[1] *Adventures of Ideas*, p. 310.

subjects. That is to say, if the eternal object, which is the predicate of a proposition, is really exemplified in the nexus, then the proposition is true. The same pattern, which is realized in the logical subjects, constituting the nexus, must appear as the predicate, if the proposition is to be true.

We should not, however, suppose that, in the case of a true proposition, since its predicate is realized in the nexus, the proposition itself becomes identified with the nexus. That is not possible. The nexus and the proposition belong to two different categories of being. The nexus is a group of actual entities and the proposition is a possibility, although its range is confined to the nexus. The proposition is a theory, a supposition, about actualities, and is not itself an actuality. The pattern occurs in the nexus in the mode of realization. It is actually embodied there. But in the proposition it stands for a possibility only, although of a limited scope. It is what may be realized in the subjects indicated. Thus the pattern, as it occurs in the proposition, has a hypothetical character, and defines a mere possibility, whereas in the nexus it defines a fact. We cannot, therefore, identify a proposition with a nexus even when the proposition is true.

For our experience, sense-perception provides the best type of appearance. The appearance we meet with here is no longer tinged with a hypothetical character. Although the sensa are derived from the bodily activities in the past, they are precipitated upon the contemporary regions, and the regions present the appearance that they are qualified by the sensa. Truth or falsity belongs to this appearance according as it conforms or does not conform to the reality. But there are different ways of conforming, direct and indirect, and in various degrees. We thus see that, although Whitehead accepts what may be called a correspondence theory of truth, he is willing to admit degrees and kinds in truth.

There is a direct conformation between the appearance and the reality—and it gives us the first species of truth—when the sensa, which qualify a region, also qualify the actual entities which make up the region. We have to recall here that the sensa are primarily ways of feeling. Our seeing of anything as red really means our feeling the thing redly. Since sensa really qualify only the modes of feeling, when they appear to qualify an external region, the question arises whether they actually qualify the affective tones of the actual entities which make up the region. If they do, then the appearance is true, because it conforms to the underlying reality.

Sense-perception may give us another species of truth, when it need not strictly correspond to the underlying reality. The sense-perception may result from the normal functionings of a healthy normal body and the body may, in its functioning, so conform to the external environment that its reactions to it are favourable to its self-preservation as well as to the preservation of the species to which it belongs. In a perception of this kind we have a truth, for we have perceived what another individual of our species would perceive under the same circumstances.

Since the perception results from the normal
functioning of a healthy normal body, it presupposes some conformation between the environment and the functions of the body.   So there
is some truth.   But the appearance may not
really reflect the actual happenings in the region
where it is seen.   Hence the truth-relation here
is less direct than in the first species.

There is yet another type of truth which may
be called symbolic.   It is the sort of truth we get
in the case of language in relation to its meaning.
There is no causal relation between the heard
sounds or visible signs on paper and the meanings
or propositions for which they stand.   There is
no direct relation between the appearance of
sights or sounds and the reality of meanings.
Still the appearance may sustain a truth-relation
if, for a properly qualified percipient, the
prehension of the appearance means the prehension of the reality : if, that is, one gets to know
the meaning by hearing or reading the language.
There is truth or falsity of this type in all kinds
of symbolism.

There may be all kinds of indirect truth with
their delicate nuances in our various experiences.
But what we really want, when we interest
ourselves in the question of truth, is the blunt
truth of the first sort, and the question at once
arises whether and how far it is available in
sense-perception.   When we see a green meadow,
and believe the appearance to be true, is it really
the case that greenness qualifies in a dominant
manner the affective tones of the actualities
which make up the meadow ?   Can the happenings within the regions of the blades of grass be

said, in any important sense, to correspond
exactly to the appearance which those regions
present to our eyes ?

It may be at once admitted that there is no
necessity that the appearance in our perception
should in every case correspond to fact.   There
are any number of cases of delusive appearance,
and they clearly show that the happenings
within the regions are oftentimes irrelevant to
their appearance.   But we need not give ourselves
up to utter scepticism.   We know that sense-
perceptions are due to our bodily functionings,
and that these functionings and the happenings
within the contemporary regions are equally
derived from a common past.   It may not be
too much to believe that our bodies are attuned
to external regions, so that under normal
conditions, our bodily functionings have their
counterparts in the happenings within those
regions, and, therefore, the appearances of those
regions, controlled as they are by our bodily
functionings, do really correspond to the actualities within the regions.   When there is perfect
adjustment between the body and the external
environment, the appearances may be true.   We
cannot, however, think that our bodies have
reached the ideal stage of perfect adjustment.
But if we look to the teleology of the universe, we
may be assured that the production of such
perfect adjustment is part of the aim of the
creative advance.

Truth by itself is no value, and is not self-
justified.   That exalted status of being something
that requires no external justification and claims
realization for its own sake, belongs to beauty.

The concept of beauty is more comprehensive than the concept of truth. Truth concerns the relation between appearance and reality. But in the case of beauty, the inter-relations of different elements of appearance, and the inter-relations of different elements of reality, as well as the relations of appearance and reality, are concerned. Truth is valuable when it subserves the purpose of beauty. And it is because truth really performs an important function in the service of beauty that it is considered valuable for its own sake. There may be a beauty concerned merely with appearance, but such beauty is shallow. When it has the harmonious backing of reality and, therefore, possesses the quality of truth, it gains in depth and effectiveness. If Whitehead is right in believing that " The teleology of the universe is directed to the production of Beauty ",[1] we may then conclude that the creative process is equally concerned in eliminating all those conditions which make for disagreement between appearance and reality, and thus in attaining greater and greater measure of truth. For the ideal beauty, which will mean all comprehensive harmony, cannot be attained while there are appearances which do not conform to reality.

---

[1] *Adventures of Ideas*, p. 341.

Chapter XII

GOD

THE concept of God is integral to the metaphysical scheme which Whitehead has propounded. God is not simply provided for in a scheme which might as well do without Him. We may very well imagine a scheme of things which would not necessarily exclude the ·idea of God but would yet be quite intelligible and consistent with itself even without God. God might have a place in such a scheme, but He would not be necessary or essential to it. It is quite otherwise with the view of reality which Whitehead presents. The picture of reality that he has depicted would be essentially incomplete, and unintelligible at many points, if God were left out of it. It is probably because he has assigned such a prominent place to God in his philosophy that many religious-minded people are drawn to it who would otherwise be repelled by the highly scientific colouring of his concepts.

Although, no doubt, God holds an eminent place in Whitehead's system, He is not above the laws and principles which regulate the other parts of the system. He is not an exception to the ultimate rules to which all beings are subject. Sometimes we have systems of philosophy which introduce the notion of God merely to tide over their inherent metaphysical difficulties. What happens mostly in such cases is that God, like a despotic ruler, administers metaphysical laws to other entities, but Himself remains outside the operation of those laws. He is made to support a system without Himself becoming a part of the system. The system works with His help, but His functions do not flow, as obligatory duties, from the system. The very reverse of this is the case with God in Whitehead's system. It is truer to say that God is supported on the system than that the system is supported on God. He does not determine how the system is to work, His functions are rather defined by the system. All this implies that God is not the ultimate principle in Whitehead's philosophy. The ultimate principle is creativity, and it is exemplified in God as well as in other actual entities.

We are trying to make out, first, that God forms an essential and necessary part of Whitehead's system, and, second, that, being an actual entity, He fulfils the general metaphysical conditions which are binding on all actual entities. These points have to be elucidated.

Let us first see how the concept of God is demanded in Whitehead's philosophy, in the light of other concepts which we have already considered. We know that the concept of eternal object is a fundamental concept in the system. The eternal objects not only determine the definiteness of things which come to be realized, but they also guide the process of their growth. They are a sort of ideals at which actual entities aim in the growth of their being. In this sense the creative evolution is guided by them.

For the explanation of an actual entity we require not only the already constituted actualities which supply its objective constitution, but also the particular possibility which guides its subjective aim and comes to be realized in it. Thus among the reasons for things, we have actual facts and possible ideals. There are final causes as well as efficient causes. But if a final cause is to be a reason at all, it must be referred to some actual entity. This is demanded by the ontological principle which says that nothing can constitute a metaphysical reason unless it can be referred to some actual entity. Whatever counts in the universe must be somewhere real. An eternal object, i.e. a possibility or an ideal, certainly does count in the universe. It is the datum of our appetitive prehension. It must therefore be somewhere real. The question now is, where should it be referred for its reality? A possibility is, of course, real in the conceptual prehension of an actual entity. But a temporal actual entity comes into being and dies away also, and along with it its conceptual prehensions also disappear. So if the eternal objects depended on temporal actual entities, they would likewise be subject to time, and would be sometimes real and sometimes unreal. But the very idea of eternal objects is that their being is not limited to any time and place. They are neither created nor destroyed by our positive or negative prehensions. A possibility remains a possibility, whether I conceive it or not. It is thus clear that if the eternal objects are to depend, as they must, on some actual entity for their reality, that actual entity must be non-temporal.

It may be supposed that all the eternal objects
one need admit are only those that actually enter
into the conceptual prehensions of temporal
actual entities, and so a non-temporal actual
entity is not necessary for them. But the very
idea of an eternal object is that it transcends in
its being the actuality of any temporal prehension.
Since it is eternal, it requires a non-temporal
actual entity for its reality.

Moreover, even for our conceptual prehension,
an eternal object must be available somewhere.
A possibility as such is not identical with any
actual fact. Where and how can we get it then ?
For us temporal beings, an idea does not float
into our prehension from nowhere. Ultimately
all the data of our experience, physical and
conceptual, are derived from our experience of
facts or actual entities. Therefore, the eternal
objects, too, must be originally realized by some
actual entity from which we can derive them.
It is, therefore, supposed that there is a primordial
actual entity, God, in whose conceptual realization all the eternal objects are given. The
primordial nature of God consists in the envisagement of all the possibilities that are realizable in
the universe.

There is another consideration. The eternal
objects have certain fixed relationships among
themselves. One eternal object is different from
another, there is diversity between them. Some
of them are similar. Apart from their realization
in some actual entity, they are mere undifferen-
tiated non-entities, and we cannot significantly
speak of them as similar to, or different from, one
another. All their relationships are significant

only in a state of realization. "The general relationships of eternal objects to each other, relationships of diversity and of pattern, are their relationships in God's conceptual realization."[1]

The above considerations are not offered in the manner of a proof for the existence of God. We are only trying to understand the meaning of an idea, and to see how it comes in the scheme of ideas which constitutes Whitehead's metaphysics. The concept of God is an item in the scheme, and one has merely to see whether the scheme as a whole serves any purpose in interpreting the facts given in one's experience.

We referred to creativity as the ultimate principle in Whitehead's philosophy. But this creativity is not by itself anything actual. In order to be actual it requires to be embodied in particular creations. And particular creations do not flow from mere general creativity as such. Creativity has to be limited in order to lead to particular creations. If we have mere general creativity and unbounded possibility, we shall never get to any actuality. General creativity has to become limited, and possibilities have to be organized or ordered, before any process of actual creation begins. Thus it is evident that some limitation must be put upon creativity if it is to become actual. The limitation is an accident, through which the ultimate principle becomes actual. Apart from the accidents, the ultimate principle has no actuality. Viewed in relation to creativity, God is regarded as "its

[1] *Process and Reality*, p. 363.

primordial non-temporal accident ".[1] God is the first creation in which creativity becomes actual.

We know every actual entity is quite determinate. The determinate character of an actual entity is partly explained by its antecedents which are also determinate. Its determination is in a way grounded in the determination of its antecedents. This is so in the case of all temporal entities.

But ultimately we must come to an actual entity, at the beginning of them all, which is not determined by anything else, because there is nothing before it. It, too, is determinate, but its determination cannot be explained. This primordial determination is ultimately the ground of all subsequent determinations, that is, of all temporal actualities, but it is itself ungrounded. This is how we understand God. He is the first actual entity which determines all other actualities but is itself undetermined by anything else.

To explain anything is to find reasons for it. And the reasons can be either the already constituted actualities, which determine the thing by way of efficient causality, or the ideal or the ideals which condition it teleologically. In both ways we are led back to God. He is the first actual entity which causally determines all other facts, and it is again He who supplies all possible ideals by His primordial envisagement of all eternal objects. We therefore refer to God for both kinds of causality, efficient and final. God's primordial nature, however, admits of no explanation, as it is not conditioned by

[1] *Process and Reality*, p. 9.

anything else. Paradoxical as it may seem, we have to admit that God is the ultimate irrationality which is the ground of all rational explanation.

From the above, we can understand how God is the principle of concretion. By being the first limitation on creativity, He makes possible all actual concrete becoming. But for Him there would be mere vague ambiguity which is neither actual in itself nor capable of giving form and direction to any concrete becoming.

We have pointed out that God is an actual entity. And, like other actual entities, He possesses a dual nature. Just as a temporal entity has a mental and a physical pole, God, too, has a mental and a physical pole, termed, in His case, the primordial nature and the consequent nature. We shall now try to understand what these natures of God mean.

" The ' primordial nature ' of God is the concrescence of a unity of conceptual feelings including among their data all eternal objects."[1] It is the envisagement by God of all the possibilities that are ever realizable in the universe. In His primordial nature, God has not merely a disinterested vision of the entire realm of eternal objects. His vision is not " free from yearning after concrete fact—no particular facts, but after some actuality ".[2] Therefore, the term envisagement is preferred to the term vision. The fact that the primordial nature of God consists of conceptual feelings shows that it involves appetition towards some realization.

---

[1] *Process and Reality*, p. 122.
[2] Ibid., p. 46.

The eternal objects are felt in such a way in God's primordial nature that they become lures of feeling for actual occasions. The conceptual feelings are valuations, and the primordial valuations of God determine " the relative relevance of eternal objects for each occasion of actuality ".[1]

In His conceptual realization, all the eternal objects have an ordered valuation, and they are graded in such a way that they are differently relevant to different occasions and have a particular relevance for each occasion. Every actual occasion, determined as it is by its objective conditions, seeks to realize some eternal objects appropriate to it. There is a demand for the realization of the relevant eternal objects in each occasion, because they have been conceived with a yearning by God. God is thus present with every occasion, supplying it with its initial subjective aim. We thus understand how, in His primordial nature, God is not before all creation but with all creation.[2] God is the beginning of all things, not in the sense of being in the past, but in the sense of being " the presupposed actuality of conceptual operation " in unison with every creative act.

Every actual occasion begins with a hybrid physical feeling of God. In this initial feeling God is felt as conceptually feeling the eternal objects, and from this is derived a conceptual feeling of some relevant eternal object, which is nothing but a yearning after an ideal. Every actual occasion thus derives its ideal from the

[1] *Process and Reality*, p. 487.
[2] Ibid., p. 486.

primordial nature of God. He is thus " the eternal urge of desire ". He is the unmoved mover. In His conceptual realization, He holds up all ideals and moves us to the realization of those that are possible for us. But in His primordial nature He is infinite and eternal, and suffers no change, because it is finally complete.

In His conceptual feelings God is not conditioned by anything at all. It is only as realized in the primordial nature of God that the eternal objects acquire an order of relevance to the creative process. But although, as conceptually realized by God, the eternal objects become relevant to the process of creation, God does not conceive them with a view to making them so relevant. God in His primordial nature has no reference to any particular creation, although His conceptual realization of eternal objects is itself a creative act which is the basis of all creation. " His unity of conceptual operations is a free creative act, untrammelled by reference to any particular course of things."[1] He has no regard or disregard for any particular thing, for nothing particular is yet in view. Considered as primordial, God is to be viewed as alone with Himself. He presupposes nothing, but is presupposed by everything.

Exalted as, no doubt, His primordial nature is, He cannot be regarded as eminently real in this aspect of His nature. It is deficient in two ways. His feelings, being merely conceptual, lack, first, the fulness of actuality, and, second, the form of consciousness. But God is not merely primordial,

[1] *Process and Reality*, p. 487.

He has His consequent nature also which fully supplies the defects of His primordial nature. Just as God is felt in every actual occasion, every actual occasion is felt back in God. This gives us His consequent nature. " The ' consequent nature ' of God is the physical prehension by God of the actualities of the evolving universe."[1] The actual world of an actual entity is felt by the actual entity and is objectified in it. The actual world of every actual entity is felt by God along with the actual entity as a novel element. God is thus the beginning and the end of things. Every actual entity, in a sense, issues from God and is received back in God.

His primordial nature is changeless, because it is finally complete ; His consequent nature grows with the creative advance of the world. The defects of His primordial nature are remedied in His consequent nature in the sense that He achieves fulness of actuality by His physical feelings of the world (which constitute His consequent nature) and becomes fully conscious by the integration of His physical feelings with His conceptual feelings. " The primordial nature is conceptual, the consequent nature is the weaving of God's physical feelings upon His primordial concepts."[2]

A temporal entity, we know, issues from some settled objective fact, and it may therefore be conceived as beginning with physical experience and completing itself through conceptual experience derived from God. God, on the other hand, begins with conceptual experience and completes

[1] *Process and Reality*, p. 122.
[2] Ibid., p. 488.

Himself by physical experience derived from the temporal world.

The reaction of the temporal world on God is His consequent nature, and in it all the actualities of the world get their adequate representation. " The truth itself is nothing else than how the composite natures of the organic actualities of the world obtain adequate representation in the divine nature."[1] All our experiences, limited and partial, get adjusted and completed in the unity of divine experience. Every actuality, evanescent in its temporal occurrence, is invested with the quality of everlastingness, when it is taken up into the consequent nature of God.

The term everlasting is used to signify the retention of immediacy with creative advance. Nothing lapses into the past for God. The consequent nature of God grows along with the evolving universe, but in the process of growth or creative advance, nothing that has once been is left behind and forgotten. All our joys and sorrows, triumphs and failures, are " woven by rightness of feeling into the harmony of the universal feeling ". Even what appears trivial and without value is revealed in its true worth in divine wisdom and retained in the immediacy of divine feeling.

The image under which this aspect of " God's nature is best conceived, is that of a tender care that nothing be lost ".[2] Another image which may help us to understand God's consequent nature is that of infinite patience. The actual course of things in the temporal world exhibits

[1] *Process and Reality*, p. 16.
[2] Ibid., p. 490.

a play of forces, both productive and destructive.
God never comes in with contrary forces of a like
nature to set matters right. The bewildering
multiplicity of created facts is absorbed and
harmonized in God's feeling with infinite patience
in the light of His perfect wisdom. " He does
not create the world, He saves it : or, more
accurately, He is the poet of the world, with
tender patience leading it by His vision of truth,
beauty and goodness."[1]

One should not forget that these are but
images, designed to give us an inkling into the
ultimate mysteries of things which are scarcely
accessible to unaided understanding. The point
to be grasped is that each temporal actuality is
received into God's nature and is transmuted
into a living ever-present fact. The fluent world
becomes " everlasting by its objective immortality
in God ". We are already familiar with the
notion of objective immortality. But objective
immortality in the temporal world means loss of
immediacy, and is not the same thing as everlastingness in God. When actuality attains
everlastingness in God, it suffers no loss, but
gains, on the contrary, completion of its nature,
by being brought, by God's feeling, into harmony
with the eternal order which is realized in God's
primordial nature, and which may be called the
final absolute " wisdom ".

We have seen that the reaction of the temporal
world on God results in His consequent nature.
The principle of relativity does not stop here.
There is a further reaction of God's consequent
nature on the temporal world according to the

[1] *Process and Reality*, p. 490.

relevance of that nature to the various concrescent occasions. Thus there are altogether four phases in the creative process in the universe. First there is the one conceptual realization of all possibilities, which is deficient in actuality, but infinite in its adjustment of valuation. Secondly, there is the physical realization of temporal actualities. In this phase there is no deficiency in actuality, but only in the solidarity of individuals with one another. This deficiency is remedied in the third phase, in which the many are united in divine feeling and are made everlasting in the consequent nature of God. In the fourth phase, the perfected actuality, achieved in the third phase, " passes back into the temporal world, and qualifies this world so that each temporal actuality includes it as an immediate fact of relevant experience ".[1] If we may conceive the consequent nature of God as the kingdom of heaven, we may say that " the kingdom of heaven is with us to-day ". " The action of the fourth phase is the love of God for the world." It provides for particular occasions in a particular way. " What is done in the world is transformed into a reality in heaven, and the reality in heaven passes back into the world. By reason of this reciprocal relation, the love in the world passes into the love in heaven, and floods back again into the world. In this sense, God is the great companion—the fellow-sufferer who understands."[2]

The problem of many and one, of flux and permanence, has been a source of unmitigated

[1] *Process and Reality*, p. 497.
[2] Ibid., p. 497.

trouble to philosophy at all times. Generally it has been held that the world is characterized by fluency and multiplicity, whereas God or the absolute has the characteristics of unity and permanence. But if these opposed characters qualify diverse actualities, their interplay at every stage will involve contradiction. Whitehead points out that there is not merely one problem of permanence and fluency, but there is a double problem here. (1) What is permanent requires fluency as its completion. (2) What is fluent requires permanence as its completion. God's primordial nature—one and permanent—requires to be completed by His consequent nature derived from the fluent multiplicity of the temporal world. And the fluent temporal world demands to be made permanent or everlasting in God's nature. We have to see that the opposed characters do not belong to separate actualities. In that case their combination would be impossible. We have, therefore, to take them as expressing different aspects of the same actuality. There is a sense in which we may speak of God as one and also as many ; and there is a sense in which we may speak of the world as one and also as many. God is one in His primordial nature, and many in His consequent nature. The world is many in temporal procession, but one in everlastingness. Similarly, God is permanent or fluent according as we understand Him in His primordial or consequent nature ; and the world, too, is fluent or permanent, according as we take it in its temporal or everlasting character. Not only these, but other opposed characters—freedom and necessity, perfection and imperfection, etc.—have to be similarly understood. "All the 'opposites' are elements in the nature of things, and are incorrigibly there. The concept of 'God' is the way in which we understand this incredible fact—that what cannot be, yet is."[1]

Process and Reality, p. 495.

Chapter XIII

SOME DIFFICULTIES

In the foregoing pages we have merely attempted to understand the main ideas of Whitehead and tried to express the same as simply as possible. We cannot pretend, however, that we have found all his ideas quite intelligible, and yet we have so far refrained from expressing our difficulties, because the purpose of the book is exposition and not criticism, and the expression of our difficulties here and there would have hampered, and not helped, the task of exposition. Moreover, an adequate discussion of all the important points in Whitehead's philosophy would demand a book to itself, much larger than the one I am attempting to write, and requiring in its writer far higher powers of metaphysical insight and critical discernment than I can ever hope to attain. Still I do not like to conceal from the reader the difficulties I myself have felt in understanding some of the main ideas of Whitehead's philosophy. I propose to state some of these difficulties in this chapter.

I take it for granted that philosophy seeks to give us knowledge, and that knowledge is always definite. The object of knowledge must be quite definite to knowledge. If we cannot say what it is that we know, we cannot be said to know it at all. This implies that the object of knowledge as object must have a completed being. If a thing is only just going to be, and is still indeterminate as to its character and being, it cannot be known in the proper sense of the term. Such a thing cannot properly find a place in philosophy, if it is the aim of philosophy to amount to knowledge.

In view of this presupposition, which may well be wrong, I find enormous difficulty in assimilating some of the fundamental ideas of Whitehead.

Let us take his most fundamental idea, creativity. Creativity is the universal of universals, and cannot therefore be understood in terms of some other concepts. All other ideas are illustrations of it, and it does not illustrate any higher concept.

Our difficulties with regard to it are twofold. First, we find it difficult even to conceive it, and if we cannot conceive it, we can far less understand other facts in terms of it. Secondly, even if it be somehow conceived, it is difficult to see how it can be an essential characteristic of all that exists.

There is a world of difference between the two positions, (i) that creativity is a mode of some being, and (ii) that every being is a mode of creativity. We can in a way understand the first position, because our thought can fix upon some being to which creativity belongs as a mode or attribute. But Whitehead maintains the second position, and it seems scarcely intelligible to thought. Creativity here is the substantive and all other beings are adjectival. What can we make of a creativity which is not subordinate to any being, but from which all beings proceed ? Since it is an ultimate notion, it should be realizable by itself. Others may depend upon it, but it should not depend upon others. But is mere creativity by itself intelligible at all? It seems that mere creativity, apart from a being which creates, is not a possible object of thought.

It may be supposed that this difficulty is of our own creation. Creativity characterizes ultimate matter of fact, and is present in everything actual, but is not anything real by itself. The ultimate metaphysical facts are the actual entities and they all exemplify creativity.

But is it, then, meant that creativity is a mere possibility and so an eternal object only? This can hardly be Whitehead's meaning. If creativity were an eternal object, it would be realized, along with other eternal objects, only in the conceptual feeling of God, and would have, therefore, no claim to being an ultimate principle. Whitehead definitely holds that God is a creature, implying thereby that God is dependent upon creativity, and so creativity cannot be an eternal object which depends for its reality on the conceptual feeling of God.

Whitehead says that creativity is " that ultimate principle by which the many, which are the universe disjunctively, become the one actual occasion, which is the universe conjunctively ".[1] He further says, " The many become one, and are increased by one."[2] Thus it appears that creativity is that principle by which the many become one, and are increased by one. But the statement, " the many become one and are increased by one ", taken literally, would be a mere paradox. When many become one, they are not increased, but only reduced to a unity.

[1] *Process and Reality*, p. 28.　　[2] Ibid., p. 29.

At least the one which the many constitute is not like one of the many which are its constituents, and so it cannot add to their number. The many can be increased by one, when that one is placed side by side with them, but the one which the many become cannot be put side by side with them, simply because they are all included in it. By the above statement, however, Whitehead merely means that the many facts of the world are united by a novel actual occasion by means of its feelings, and the novel entity, after the attainment of its satisfaction, is added as another fact to the other facts of the world. But this does not seem to add much to the intelligibility of the notion of creativity. We do not understand what it exactly is and how it leads to any actual creation.

Supposing that we understand what is meant by creativity, do we then find it illustrated in every actual thing of the world ? The actual entities are the ultimate metaphysical facts, and if creativity is to be found anywhere, it must be found in them. But do we actually find it there ? An actual entity is constituted by a subjective unity of feeling in which certain objective data are felt. The subjective feeling is not creative ; it merely feels the objective data. The objective data, as elements in the objective constitution of an actual entity, are not actual by themselves, and so cannot be credited with any creative function.

It may be supposed that the subject arises out of the objective data, and it leads other subjects beyond itself, and in this sense there is creativity everywhere.

But when a subject leads to another subject beyond itself, it becomes an object to the latter, and so this comes to mean that the objects create the subject. And since the object as object is real only within the unity of a subject, to say that the object creates the subject is to say that the subject creates itself. To us, the idea of a thing creating itself seems hopelessly unintelligible. It is true that in philosophy we are familiar with the notion of substance which is described as its own cause. But this means in plain language that a substance has no cause, and involves no idea of a creative activity in which both creator and created are one. The idea of a substance having no cause involves no contradiction, whereas the idea of a thing being both creator and created in respect of the same creative act involves self-contradiction.

Whatever else creativity may or may not do, it certainly binds together two entities (the creator and the created) in a continuous process. When creativity is taken to be the fundamental character of all things, we are compelled to suppose that everything is continuous with something else. This position seems scarcely compatible with the idea that the actual entities are all atomic in character, that is, divided from one another.

It seems that knowledge of anything will not be possible, if we make creativity absolutely universal. For to know anything as it really is, we have to know it as creative, that is to say, in relation to something else, and that something, also being creative, will lead us beyond itself, and we shall thus be led on to an infinite process, since by hypothesis there is nothing which is uncreative and with which we can stop. As we cannot complete an infinite process, we cannot know anything definitely. This difficulty presents itself more explicitly in connection with the idea of an actual entity.

An actual entity does not exist by itself. It includes other actual entities in its objective constitution, and it enters in its turn into the constitution of other actual entities. This is demanded by the principle of relativity, which Whitehead advocates, repudiating the absolutist notion of substance having its own private quality. But how is such an actual entity to be known at all ? In order to know it in its proper character, we must know the others as well which enter into it, but these others, to be known, will lead us beyond themselves to other actual entities, and we do not know how or where we can stop. This means that we cannot complete a single thought and arrive at a definite knowledge of anything. Our knowledge cannot fix upon anything at all, because by the inherent relativity of things, it is found to be led away from whatever it may try to make its object. Where everything is, for its being and character, indebted to something else, we cannot say that anything has a completed being. This is surely an intolerable situation from the point of view of knowledge, because knowledge demands completed being in its object, and where everything is essentially incomplete, knowledge has no scope.

It may be supposed that, although knowledge in our sense may not be possible in a situation where everything is essentially relative, the relativity of things may still be a fact. But even this we cannot properly understand. If everything is relative, the idea of relativity itself will collapse. If a thing is nothing in itself, we cannot say that it is relative, because the term " it " is significant only when it stands for one definite being by itself, and no such being is admitted by the theory under consideration.

It may be said that although an entity is not anything by itself, others may make it what it is. But what about these others ? If these others are granted to have being in themselves, then the theory of universal relativity is given up. If they have no such being, they cannot be the source of being for something else, and we must seek for it elsewhere. Either, then, we shall get to things which enjoy being in themselves and can therefore impart it to others, in which case the theory of relativity will have to be given up ; or we shall get to no such things, and nothing will be able to realize itself. If the consequence of the theory of relativity is that nothing should be real, we can hardly believe that it states a fact. Just as we cannot believe that an association of beggars can raise a capital by mutual borrowing, we find it difficult to understand how anything can be real where nothing is real in itself. Unless we can believe in the impossible metaphysical feat of generating facts out of mere relations, we cannot believe that everything is essentially relative to, or real through, something else.

It is true, however, that in Whitehead's philosophy everything is not really relative. The individuality of an actual occasion, as enjoying a unique unity of feeling, is quite absolute. " The individual immediacy of an occasion is the final unity of subjective form, which is the occasion as an absolute reality."[1] An actual entity is nothing if it is not an individual and its individuality consists in the form of its subjective feeling. In its individual self-enjoyment, an actual entity seems to be above all relativity. What is the truth, then, about the actual entity? Is it an absolute individual, above and outside the network of social relations which bind together all objects? Or is it of a nature that its very being consists in such relations?

It may be supposed that an actual entity is quite unique as a subjective feeling, but as an objective fact it is related to everything else. And since an actual entity is both subject and object, it is absolute as well as relative.

But what is meant by an actual entity being both subject and object? It may mean (i) that an actual entity includes both subjective and objective factors or (ii) that an actual entity is subject in relation to some entities which condition its being, and object in relation to others which are conditioned by it. Both these meanings are in a sense true of all actual entities as described by Whitehead. But none of them seems to justify us strictly to speak of an actual entity as both subject and object, or to provide any legitimate escape from our difficulty. If an actual entity includes both subjective and objective factors, it should be understood as inclusive of them both, and in that case it cannot be spoken of as both subject and object, for what

[1] *Adventures of Ideas*, p. 227.

includes them both is not surely either of them, and if it is neither, it cannot be both. But if it is neither subject nor object, what can it be then ? Let us, therefore, suppose that it is a subjective unity in which the object is included as a factor. If we are right in thus understanding the nature of an actual entity, then it will not be true to say that it is both subject and object. We have to recognize that it is merely a feeling subject, and in its subjectivity it is quite absolute, because in its immediacy of subjective feeling it is not determined by anything else.

But it may be argued here that through its objective content the subject is related to all that has gone before it, and when it is itself turned into an object, it gets related to other subjects which are conditioned by it.

This argument, too, does not solve our difficulty. The objective content, whatever it is, is included in the subjective feeling which knows nothing beyond itself. When the subjective feeling arises, it arises with its objective content, and there is no question of its being related to other pre-existent subjects or actual entities, because they are already dead, and have passed into objective immortality. From this it is also evident that the subject cannot get related to other subjects by turning itself into an object. Because, as its being is defined by subjectivity, when it ceases to be a subject, it ceases to exist, and we can no longer speak of its being related to anything else. We cannot speak of an actual entity when it is no longer actual, and it certainly ceases to be actual when it reaches its satisfaction and falls down exhausted and dead. Thus it appears misleading and untrue to say that the subject becomes an object or that an actual entity, which is a subjective unity of feeling, becomes also an objective content in other actual entities.

Whitehead clearly says, " Actual entities perish, but do not change ; they are what they are."[1] If actual entities merely arise and perish, and if they are the ultimate metaphysical facts, then we have merely momentary particulars, each absolute in itself. We cannot, then, understand how there can be any inheritance from occasion to occasion. When an actual entity perishes, we cannot say that a part of it remains to be carried over into other actual entities, because a part of an actual entity, not being an actual entity itself, is nothing at all, since actual entities are the ultimate metaphysical facts. Thus it appears that when an actual entity perishes, it disappears altogether and can leave no legacy for its successors.

If we choose to understand being in terms of life, what is not living will have to be taken as no being at all. Similarly, when we take the actual entities to be the ultimate metaphysical facts, what is not an actual entity will have to be taken as no fact. If this is so, then it is extremely difficult to understand what Whitehead means when he speaks of " settled fact " or " objective immortality ". His settled fact seems to be no fact, and his objective immortality appears to be enjoyed by actual entities only when they are no longer actual and are reduced to nothing.

[1] *Process and Reality*, p. 48.

It may be asked whether we have no meaning for objective data ; and that is really a point that requires to be cleared up. We are told, no doubt, that the subject arises out of the objective data, and is conditioned by them. But what can possibly be the nature of these data which condition the subject transcendent to them ? We can think of them as " the already constituted actual entities ". But there is a difficulty here. Since these actualities must have already attained their satisfaction, they should be dead when the new creature, beyond them, begins its career. And if we are right in thinking that an actual entity leaves no remainder when it perishes, we do not exactly see what the objective data can be which are to condition the actual entity coming after them.

It may be supposed that the objective data are not necessarily the dead actualities in which the process of feeling is already extinct. They may be actual entities in the real sense of the term with the spark of feeling still alive in them.

But actual entities as actual are merely themselves, and we have no reason to think of them as objective data. They are objective data only in relation to the subject which is transcendent to them. The actual entities get the status of objective data, so it seems, when the creative process has advanced beyond them, and they are no longer the centres of immediate feeling. When the immediacy of feeling has passed beyond them, we cannot but suppose that the former actual entities are no longer actual.

It may be objected that we are emphasizing only the subjective side of an actual entity, and

are forgetting that it must have an objective
side also, without which it cannot be complete.
And we may at once admit that our difficulty
precisely concerns the objective side of an actual
entity.   Since an actual entity can be felt only
when it is past, and has presumably ceased to be
actual, we do not see how, when it has ceased to
be actual, it is still anything at all that can be
felt.   And if it does not cease to be actual even
when it is past, there is no reason why it should
ever perish.

It may be argued that, although a thing is not
actual apart from a process of feeling, an actual
entity does not become unreal when it loses the
immediacy of feeling, because it can be real as an
element in some other feeling.   The point of this
argument seems to be that what dies as a feeling
subject may still live as a felt object.   But when
a feeler as feeler has perished, in what sense can
we say that it still persists as a felt object ?   There
is no means of effecting or proving an identity
between the feeler and the felt nor of extracting
a common element out of them both.   If this
is not possible, if the subject cannot be the same
thing as the object, we can hardly maintain that
when an actual occasion suffers subjective death,
it still enjoys objective immortality.

Every actuality is supposed to have a formal
and an objective constitution.   Formally it is
a private subjective feeling, and objectively it is
a public fact.   But how is the unity of the two
sides ever to be realized ?   How can we know
that the two sides belong to one and the same
thing ?   Can we significantly speak of one and
the same thing as both private and public

without laying ourselves open to the charge of self-contradiction ?

We have difficulties also with regard to the conception of eternal objects. They are spoken of as pure potentials and are supposed to be realized only in conceptual prehensions. But they are also exemplified in actual facts. What is the meaning of their exemplification ? What exactly is the relation between the actual fact and the eternal object which it exemplifies ? We cannot say that both become one, because they belong to two different categories of being, and one cannot absorb the other without falsifying its nature. And yet somehow they must be in a mode of unity if the one is to exemplify the other.

Whitehead sometimes speaks of an eternal object exemplified in a nexus as occurring in a mode of realization. Is there any difference between such realization and realization in a conceptual feeling ? There seems to be some difference between an eternal object as it is realized in a conceptual feeling and the same eternal object as it is realized in an actual entity or in a nexus. But we hardly know what that difference is.

Eternal objects are also described as forms of definiteness. Everything actual is definite. There is no indefinite actuality. Definiteness is the soul of actuality. If this is so, then it is difficult to distinguish the definiteness of an actual thing from the actual thing itself. At least it will have to be conceded that everything actual appears in the guise of some eternal object. If we still think of an eternal object as a mere possible, we have to say that possibility is the form of actuality. But the terms in such a statement hardly convey any consistent meaning. The ungiven character of a possibility appears incapable of being combined with the givenness of actuality. The idea of possibility seems to be different from that of definiteness, and we are not sure whether they can be legitimately combined in a single concept.

The eternal objects are not unrelated among themselves. On the contrary, each of them occupies a definite place in the realm of eternal objects, and is supposed to be internally related to all the rest. If this is so, then it appears impossible to isolate one eternal object from all others, so that when an actual thing exemplifies one eternal object, it will have to exemplify all the others as well. The whole realm of eternal objects will have to be present in everything.

Whitehead himself seems to realize this difficulty. But he tries to get over it by supposing that an eternal object has an individual and a relational essence, and that although an eternal object is internally related to others, the relata (eternal objects) are not taken in their individual essence, but only in their relational essence. But can we really make such a distinction between the individual and the relational essence? If the individual essence of a term does not come out in its relationships, we can hardly say that the term possessing the individual essence is related at all. Moreover, to say that a term is related merely in its relational essence is as good as to say that the relationships themselves constitute the term.

When we come to consider the concept of feeling, we find ourselves confronted with similar difficulties. Whitehead has certainly done a great thing in bringing under one conception what goes on in the inanimate world as well as what passes between conscious individuals. His term feeling or prehension is useful in indicating the specific character of actual relations that take place between actual things. But with all its merits, if it is to be intelligible, it must be understood after the analogy of some aspect of our own experience. And we seem to find no clear analogue in our experience to what Whitehead describes as a feeling. Nowhere do we find anything like a feeling hurled beyond a feeler, waiting to be appropriated by a subject, which it partly constitutes, but which has yet to arise. The concrescence of an actual entity is a complex process. From some objective data several feelings arise one after another and they all together, by integration and supplementation, constitute a complex unity which is an actual entity. The actual entity is constituted by all the feelings, and so in the earlier stages, when there are other constituent feelings yet to arise, the actual entity cannot be said to be there at all. We are therefore obliged to think that there can be a feeling which is not yet in any actual entity. But this we cannot obviously understand. A feeling, or anything like a feeling, is intelligible only as entertained by an actual feeler or subject. But a feeling shooting out in the air and waiting for the generation of its feeler appears more or less as an absurdity to ordinary understanding.

It may be contended that the same subject is

present throughout one unitary process, so that
no constituent feeling is without its feeler. But
if the subject arises with the first feeling, how is it
to be distinguished from the feeling itself? How,
again, is the identity of the subject as present in
different feelings to be established or understood ?
Moreover, if each feeling is completed with its
subject, what need is there for it to be integrated
with others, and what do all feelings accomplish
by such integration? Whitehead clearly says
that there is incomplete subjective unity in the
earlier stages. If one is right in thinking that
the subject is not real without unity, may not one
then suppose that there is really no subject in the
earlier stages ?

Even in the completed stage, the actual entity,
which comprehends all the constituent feelings,
is conceived as a unity of feeling. But the unity
of feeling is but the feeling as one, and by its
unity we do not get to anything, other than the
feeling, or different from it in metaphysical
character. We have to say, then, that feeling
is the feeler. We are thus required to understand
an activity in which nothing is active or the
activity is the actor. We know this way of
thinking agrees well with certain respectable
schools of thought, but we can hardly imagine
that this would be acceptable to ordinary thought.

It may be supposed that the subject is not
posterior to the feelings but it arises along with
them, and so, just as the subject is not real apart
from the particular feelings, each particular
feeling is not also real by itself, and hence there is
no difficulty, since they are all real only in a
concrete unity which is the real subject.

But we have elaborate descriptions of the derivation of feelings, one from another, and of their integration, all falling within one unity. We cannot possibly conceive that derivation and integration take place in a world of unreality, and we get all at once to the unified reality. If this were the case, we should get merely atomic realities, allowing no process within themselves. This would be inconsistent with Whitehead's main thesis.

There are difficulties with regard to the conception of God, too. The primordial nature of God is said to consist in the envisagement of all eternal objects. But since this envisagement lacks consciousness, we cannot properly say that God in His primordial nature has a vision of all possibilities. We are therefore left with blind appetency, and it is extremely difficult to conceive how the infinite possibilities, realizable in the universe, are to be represented in this blind feeling.

This nature is supposed to be eternal and unchanging, because it is finally complete. But when the possibilities come to be realized, does it make no difference to the appetition which yearns after their realization? The realization of a possibility yearned after should mean the satisfaction of the yearning, and satisfaction should make some difference to it. Longing or appetition is unintelligible apart from a demand for satisfaction, and if satisfaction means a change, we have to say that it is incompatible with God's primordial nature. Thus it appears that God in this aspect of His nature is only an eternal longing (whatever it may mean) which demands satisfaction, but from the nature of the case can never find it.

This nature lacks fulness of actuality as well as consciousness. These defects are supposed to be remedied by His consequent nature. The consequent nature of God consists in the physical prehensions of the temporal actualities of the world. But how or where are these actualities to be had ? They have no being prior to the being of God. Since they can arise only by initially feeling physically other actualities, it is apparent that God must already be actual, if there are to be any actualities at all. Thus we find that the temporal actualities cannot realize themselves unless God is already actual, and God cannot actualize Himself unless the temporal actualities are there. We do not know how we can get over this difficulty.

Again, all things are said to be harmonized in the consequent nature of God. But there are all sorts of incompatible things in the world, and God takes the " care that nothing be lost ". How, in that case, are they harmonized also ? God does not forcibly set matters right in the world. He does not bring into play any productive or destructive force, but by the rightness of feeling harmonizes all things. But the difficulty is to see how objective wrong can be righted by subjective feeling. Whitehead himself says, it appears quite truly, that " The concept of God is the way in which we understand the incredible fact that what cannot be, yet is."[1] We like merely to add that it is not quite *understandable* " that what cannot be, yet is ".

[1] *Process and Reality*, p. 495.

The nature of God is frankly admitted to be inexplicable. There is absolutely no reason why there should be a God or a God of the description Whitehead has supplied. Can we, then, characterize the whole system, with such a big irrational element in it, as rational ?

Our difficulty throughout has been, firstly, with the inherent dualism at every step. Subject and object, physical pole and mental pole, primordial nature and consequent nature, are, each pair, no doubt, said to stand for the two aspects of the same thing. But we are not provided with any unifying principle which would clearly show their internal unity.

Secondly we are troubled by the way of thought which dominates the whole system, but which seems to run counter to our ordinary thinking. Our ordinary thought operates with substantive terms with adjectival relations ; in Whitehead we find relations supplying the terms. Our thought demands facts with completed being, but in Whitehead transitional functions are offered for standing facts, and therefore our thought seems to find no foothold. Probably with Bradley and Bergson, Whitehead should say that thought is inadequate to grasp the nature of reality.

Chapter XIV

CONCLUSION

WE stated some of our difficulties in the last chapter. But it would be wrong to suppose that they tend to undermine the value of Whitehead's philosophy. The difficulties have been real enough to us, and probably they will occur to others as well. But they may well be due to our traditional habits of thought or even to our inadequate understanding of the principles of Whitehead's philosophy. We have not the slightest doubt that Whitehead has been guided, in his philosophical thought, by a deep intuition of reality, which has lent meaning and evidence to his arguments. In all probability our difficulties proceed ultimately from the lack of that intuition, and so our complaint is that he has not clearly shown how one can arrive at that intuition or grasp it in terms of ordinary thought. His master-idea is creativity or process, which no one can possibly ignore if he remains faithful to experience. The question is whether it can be made absolute and, if it is made absolute, whether it still remains accessible to thought. There have been other thinkers in the history of philosophy, who have made evolutionary process essential to their absolute or have made the process itself absolute. But they have either appealed to a " higher " thought, which is very different from ordinary thought, or rejected thought altogether as a means of philosophic knowledge. Whitehead has done neither ; he has not postulated any higher thought or any other peculiar organ of philosophic knowledge. And so the expectation is that what he says will be intelligible to ordinary thought, but the expectation at many critical steps remains unfulfilled. It is quite possible, however, that the difficulties will disappear with a change in our habits of thought or with a deeper understanding of Whitehead's ideas.

But even if there are many real difficulties inherent in his system—and Whitehead will not certainly claim that he has given the final system of philosophy free from all difficulties—they should not make us blind to its great merits. In Whitehead's philosophy we have a synthesis of knowledge that is scarcely to be met with elsewhere in contemporary philosophy. One cannot but admire the vast sweep of his mind which not only commands the different branches of contemporary knowledge, scientific and other, but shows easy familiarity with the ideas of the great leaders of thought, ancient, medieval and modern, so far at least as the Western world is concerned. He has pressed all his wonderful knowledge into the service of philosophic speculation. There is probably no other contemporary philosopher who is so well acquainted with the results of the sciences or has made such use of his scientific knowledge in philosophic interest. And with all this, he makes no display of superior knowledge, but shows everywhere an anxiety to bring his ideas into line with those of other thinkers.

He has taken into consideration all the relevant facts of philosophic importance and has sought to do justice to all sides of human experience. He has not constructed his philosophy merely on the data supplied by science, but the facts of moral and religious life have made their contribution in shaping his ideas. Coming within philosophy proper, it is evident that he has tried not to allow himself to be swayed by one school of thought. Thus we find, although on the whole the temper of his philosophy is realistic, many of his ideas are in consonance with idealistic tenets. His repudiation of the doctrine of " vacuous actuality " easily reminds one of the idealist's rejection of the independent object unrelated to experience.

He has taken care not to emphasize one side to the neglect of others. He has tried to combine being with becoming, permanence with change, mind with matter, unity with multiplicity. Although his ultimate principle is a process of becoming, it results in concrete facts which possess completed being. Nothing is static, and in this sense there is change everywhere, but every actual occasion is fixed in its spatio-temporal position, and so does not change. Every actual entity is mind as well as matter. It is matter in its physical feelings of other actualities, and it is mind in its conceptual valuations of possible ideals. Every actuality, again, is one as well as many ; it is unique and impartible in its subjective individuality, but multiple in its objective constitution. We cannot say how far he has succeeded in effecting a real synthesis of these opposed elements, and how far he has achieved final results in his great endeavour. But there is absolutely no doubt that he has tried to fulfil his great task of a constructive philosopher in a grand manner, in right temper, with requisite knowledge and patience.

He has not been content to give us merely broad general concepts derived from imagination or insight. But he has with infinite patience worked out the details of his system and has indicated their bearing on diverse facts of life. If philosophy is philosophizing, one is bound to admit that Whitehead is really a great philosopher apart from whatever verdict posterity may come to pronounce upon his system. The value of a philosopher's work is to be measured not merely by the results it offers, but especially by the manner in which the work is carried out. Whitehead's work is certainly very valuable in showing how in philosophy broad-based generalizations have to be combined with minute analysis, and in demonstrating what balance and restraint it is necessary for a philosopher to bring to bear on his work. He has indeed given us a very fine example of a calm thinker who is anxious to do justice to both sides of a question and ready to accommodate divergent facts within a theory, and who is unwilling to be carried away by a line of thought that would compel him in the end to court some kind of illusionism to escape from the consequences of onesided thinking.

It is true that Whitehead's principal metaphysical work is not particularly rich in logical arguments leading to definite conclusions. There are certainly many subtle arguments interspersed in the book, but they are subsidiary. But it has to be remembered that a philosophical system is not arrived at as the result of a logical argument, as the conclusion of an inference. Whitehead's method is frankly descriptive. He has tried to explain the basic ideas of his system, and has shown in many places their applications, too. For this, not much logical reasoning is necessary. We have to see, first, whether we can grasp these ideas by sympathetic imagination, and then, whether they are useful in interpreting the facts we meet with in life.

It would have been better, of course, if he had clearly shown in every case how and from what data of common experience he arrived at his philosophic conclusions. Our difficulties with his writings would have been far less if we always knew from what commonly accepted facts he started and what intelligible line of reasoning he followed to gain his results. But although he has not given us this help, we can never mistake the fact that he has meditated deeply on vital philosophical problems, and anybody who has himself struggled with these problems cannot easily miss the significance of Whitehead's conclusions. If one is not satisfied with any of Whitehead's conclusions, one will at least realize how extremely difficult it is to offer anything which is more satisfactory or which does better justice to all sides of the question.

When science is tending to absorb the intellectual interest of all mankind, and is being recognized, even by non-scientists, to be the only real knowledge, Whitehead, familiar as he is with the results of modern science, has courageously shown the limitations of scientific knowledge. He has shown how science, far from being the embodiment of truth itself, gives us but half-truths, when its results are not co-ordinated and supplemented, and so, modified, by more comprehensive metaphysics. When metaphysics is looked upon with distrust by many and its very possibility is disputed by some, Whitehead has rendered a signal service to the cause of pure thought by demonstrating not only the possibility but also the necessity and great value of metaphysical speculation. At least on this account, if not for anything else, all students of philosophy have reason to be grateful to him.

He does not, however, repudiate science. He is not untrue to its spirit nor forgetful of its great service. Not only does he not reject the evidence of science, but he makes all possible use of it in framing philosophical concepts as also in solving philosophical problems. This is to be expected of a thinker whose mind is so full of scientific ideas. His actual entity, although very similar to a Leibnizian monad, is more like an atom of science. The process of feeling, which is his central theme, appears to be a transfiguration of the flow of energy with which science deals. While trying to solve the epistemological problem of perception, he does not neglect the teachings of physics and physiology.

He no doubt speaks of scientific ideas as abstractions, but the more concrete philosophical concepts which he offers were probably formulated in the light of scientific ideas. The scientific origin of his philosophical ideas is shown more or less clearly by his explicit references to science in his philosophical writings. His anxiety to show how his ideas agree with philosophical tradition shows in a way that they were not probably originally derived from this tradition. But, whatever their origin, there is no doubt about their genuineness as philosophical concepts. It will not, therefore, be inappropriate to say that in Whitehead science has found its philosopher and philosophy its scientist.

Others have also spoken of scientific ideas as abstractions, but Whitehead's assertion in this regard is more significant in that he also points out the more concrete forms from which the scientific ideas are abstractions. He points out, for instance, that " The notion of physical energy which is at the base of physics, must then be conceived as an abstraction from the complex energy, emotional and purposeful, inherent in the subjective form of the final synthesis in which each occasion completes itself."[1]

We cannot predict what permanent influence the writings of Whitehead will have on the future of philosophy, and do not really know whether there are in his philosophy germs of ideas that will give an altogether new direction to philosophy. But we certainly know that he has attempted to solve many vexed problems of philosophy, and some originality and plausibility may really be claimed for his solutions. And we also know that he has drawn attention to many facts which are generally overlooked, but which, when properly appreciated, tend to change the aspect of many philosophical problems.

[1] *Adventures of Ideas*, p. 239.

Thus, for instance, we have been accustomed to think that our five senses are the only gates of knowledge, and even among them we have given undue importance to the eyes, so that in current discussions on the sensa the visual sensa are mostly taken into consideration. Whitehead rightly points out the fact that " the living organ of experience is the living body as a whole ".[1] We are in contact with the world through our whole body, and not merely through certain parts of it only. And any activity in any part of the body is as good a source of genuine experience as any activity of the sense-organs.

In their speculation about the nature of the world, philosophers have mostly depended on sense-perception, and that, too, in the mode of presentational immediacy. Whitehead has earned our sincere gratitude by laying great emphasis on another side of our experience, which is deeper than the experience of presentational immediacy, and is described by him as the feeling of causal efficacy. When we rely merely on presentational immediacy, it is possible to believe that the world is a mere appearance, because presentational immediacy by itself does not acquaint us with any actuality behind the appearance. In a causal feeling, however, we are unmistakably aware of the compelling force of an actuality external to ourselves. If the value and significance of the causal feelings, on which Whitehead has insisted so much, comes to be properly appreciated, the kind of view which says that the world is a mere appearance will cease to interest mankind.

[1] *Adventures of Ideas*, p. 289.

It is yet an unsolved problem whether reality belongs ultimately to the object or to the subject. The object is the pillar of strength to realism, and idealism draws its sustenance from the resources of the subject. The one emphasizes the object, the other the subject. Whitehead has tried to lay due emphasis on both. He emphasizes the subject in that he holds that an actual entity is, after all, a unity of subjective experience. He emphasizes the object in that he makes the subject derivative from the object.

Whether freedom or necessity rules the world is another standing problem of philosophy. Whitehead has tried to solve this problem by accommodating both freedom and necessity within every actual entity. An actual entity is determined by its past. The past or the actual entities out of which it arises cannot but be felt by it, and so there is necessity, but how they are to be felt is left to the actual entity itself, and hence there is freedom. We are born in bondage, but grow in freedom. There is objective necessity, but there is also subjective freedom.

INDEX

DATE DUE

GAYLORD			PRINTED IN U.S.A.